Speak Life

... and shut the hell up!

BEV MURRILL

RIVER
PUBLISHING

River Publishing & Media Ltd
Barham Court
Teston
Maidstone
Kent
ME18 5BZ
United Kingdom

info@river-publishing.co.uk

ISBN 978-1-908393-18-0
Printed in the United Kingdom

Contents

Dedication

This book is dedicated to Rick Murrill, my loving, faithful and patient best friend. Together we have risen to the challenge of 40 years of married life and have seen His strength perfected in our weakness. Rick's initial revelation of the power of speaking life changed our life.

This book is also dedicated to all those, both within and without the Murrill Tribe and the CGI network, who have discerned and valued our stumbling attempts to learn to speak and operate out of an understanding of the language of life and who, in observing our efforts, have reasoned that if we can do it, it must not be an impossible task.

Thank you to those who have spoken life to us and those who have determined to learn to speak life into their own worlds. Your faith and belief in proliferating the language of life has encouraged us more than you can possibly know.

Finally, this book is dedicated to our rapidly increasing herd of grandchildren who are the delight of our lives and whom we pray will become fluent life speakers and remain so all the days of their lives.

Meekah Angel, Caelan Amber, Echo Jazmine Tobin, Tahlei Rosie, Tekoa Daniel, Leland Charles, Anyssa Alice ,

...and the two who are currently still cooking ... and those who are still only known to the plan of God. There's bound to be more of them — they're coming thick and fast.

Thanks to Julie Gardiner, Trevor Waldock and Chrissie Kelly for their insights into Jesus' radical decision to unveil his intentions for the future Church at the Gates of Hell.

Foreword

The story of humanity is the story of language. Community is built on communication, and the choices we make about how we speak express something of the very heart of who we are. And yet we think so little about the words we use. Are there languages open to us that are more constructive, more useful, more conducive to life than others? Do the words that fill our minds and form our speech have the power to change the world around us?

Rick and Bev Murrill believe that they do. Both Australians, they came to the UK in 1996 to take on the leadership of a baptist church in Essex. That first church is now the thriving "Christian Growth Centre", Chelmsford, and a host of other churches have been planted or renewed. The Murrills have founded "Christian Growth International" to oversee this network, which now includes churches in the USA and a remarkable project amongst AIDS orphans in Uganda. More than this, Rick and Bev have mentored a generation of younger leaders who are themselves now achieving great things in church leadership, social action and entrepreneurial projects. There is a time-honoured biblical tradition that true leadership shows itself by its fruits, and Rick and Bev's stature is seen in the many, many people who will speak of them with unwavering honour and gratitude.

Key to their journey is a concept they have called "speaking life": a way of harnessing and disciplining language as a servant of the purposes of God. This is the spiritual practise at the heart of Rick and Bev's ministry, and it is this approach that has most influenced the churches they have shaped and the leaders they have mentored. In *Speak Life... and Shut the Hell Up*, Bev distills the lessons learned over these many years to capture the essence of the "speaking life" concept. Drawing lessons from sources as diverse as David before Goliath, Ezekiel in his valley of dry bones and Chicken Licken spreading panic through the farmyard, Bev urges us to learn and practise the "language of life". This is God's language; language that casts out both fear and denial and moves, rather, towards faith.

This makes for an important and challenging book. We all use language. Words are at the heart of who we are. Which of us cannot benefit from reflecting on how we use words? I have been personally challenged through this material and have had cause to re-visit ingrained ways of thinking, of speaking and of praying. I have tested the concept of "speaking life" and have seen changes flowing from it. If you will take this book on trust, and let it speak to who you are, I believe it has the potential to change you. What better recommendation could there be for a book on the spiritual life?

A word of warning is perhaps appropriate here. Language is the subject of this book but, ironically, the language of the book itself may send a false signal to some. The practises of "positive thinking" and "faith confession" are often presented in words not unlike those offered here. But don't be deceived by this. "Speaking life isn't merely positive speaking," Bev writes, "nor is it a 'name it and claim it' brand of fake faith which often masks a tendency to live in denial. Speaking life relates to the deepest parts of who we are and how our hearts communicate – with the world, with each other, and with God." This is an important distinction and reflects the depth of study and prayer that have gone into the crafting of this material. Reading this book will challenge the way you think and the way you pray; the language you use to describe your circumstances and the ways you communicate with others. May it bear abundant fruit in many of us, teaching us to speak as God would have us speak, and empowering us to surf the waves of life God surely longs to bring to our churches and communities.

Gerard Kelly
Bethanie, France
January 2012

Preface

"Truth has no special time of its own; its hour is now ... always."
~Albert Schweitzer

Yes, I know. It's a pretty outrageous name for a Christian book. But if you manage to get past the name and read the rest of it, you will find that, far from swearing, this is a book that means what it says on the cover!

Hell has a language all of its own and its voice into society articulates all the negativity, evil and brokenness of the world we live in. When Christians understand the concept of *speaking the life of Christ* into their own spheres, however, they will discover that they have the power to shut hell, with all its influence, down also.

The day a person becomes a Christian they are not only infused with the life of Christ, but are also entrusted with a deposit of the Kingdom of Heaven to take with them wherever they go. It's our privilege and responsibility to plant and nurture the Kingdom where we work, play, live and engage with the rest of the world, just like Jesus did. He was not afraid to be seen in the places where (what others deemed to be) the riff raff of society hung out. His purpose there was to bring in the Kingdom. That same divine nature takes His place in us with the same intention.

That divine incarnation within us enables and equips us to be His agents of change in the spheres of influence we inhabit, whether we are among the rich or poor, the socially acceptable or not. We were created not just with the capacity and propensity for a relationship with God, but to be bearers of His Kingdom wherever we go. As with Tolkein's unlikely hero, Frodo the Ring Bearer, this is a weighty responsibility and despite our willingness to do it, we are deeply aware of our lack in the area of the power, confidence, energy or wisdom to do what we've been called to do.

Fear and anxiety, arrogance and selfishness, shame and condemnation all dog our steps as we haltingly make the journey, our faith at times overwhelmed by the sheer magnitude of the giants and wild beasts we encounter as we go ... and that's just on the inside of us, without even starting on what we meet up with outside our own hearts.

Since the dominion of the earth was given over to Satan in Eden, the world has suffered from an obsession with death. It's not just in the wars and attacks that abound, it's in the way we speak and the way we treat each other day to day. Racism, sex trafficking, gender prejudice, paedophilia, riots, legalism, pollution, even many of our sports and computer games, are all facets of the death which pervades our planet. Each of these things are framed and established as legitimate philosophies by the words used to express them. Those ugly beliefs begin in our hearts, which inform our thoughts, which direct our words. Our words influence those around us and develop into actions, and those combined actions form the atmospheres that dictate the behaviour and belief systems of the societies we live in.

Jesus came to give us abundant life, but even Christians tend to adapt to their societies' viewpoints, embracing all manner of ungodly values and eroding that abundance until the decay and detritus of our potential to transform our world is often all that is left visible.

There are all sorts of reasons why Kingdom bearers don't make the choice to engage the Kingdom of God in our daily life, bringing it with us into our spheres of influence. The primary reason, however, is because we have been enculturised into a society that finds such a concept bizarre and incomprehensible and we have little confidence in our capacity to do it.

We lose sight of the fact that we cannot do it in our own strength; the power of the Holy Spirit is there to enable us, just as His command is for us to do it. Literally, if we will do what only we can do, which involves ordering our words in accordance with His words, we release Him to do what only He can do.

Even people who have the life of God infused into every cell can often still be trapped in and by their culture. Our language is more inclined to emulate that of the society around us, rather than adopting the language of the One who spoke the world into being. We also speak our world into being, but it's not the one we want … and it's not the plan of God.

We tend more towards speaking the language of death as our conversation repeatedly highlights our anxieties, our hopelessness, our depression and rejection, denying, by our neglect and unbelief, the true power of His Word; the power of God to change our situation and the world around us.

Truth is not relative, it's specific and focused in every situation, but the revelation of truth is selective and it is we who select it. When God's people learn His *language of life* that encapsulates and establishes the potential He sees in us, an outbreak of Heaven is the result. Change is birthed. Peace ensues. Atmospheres are altered. Families are healed and economies revived.

Changing the way we speak is not an easy thing. It entails intentionality, effort and understanding. Learning the language of God is no different to learning any other language, but the reward for doing so is mind blowing. You have no idea how much your own words have been condemning your future and that of the people you love, and you have no idea, until you make a beginning, just how much you can change your future by changing the way you speak of it and yourself.

Every Christian is called to use their life to usher in the Kingdom of God. Learning God's language is vital for everyone who takes that commission seriously.

"In Him was Life, and the Life was the Light of men. And the Light shines on in the darkness, for the darkness has never overpowered it." (John 1:4-5 Amp)

*"It is the Spirit who gives life; the flesh is no help at all.
The words that I have spoken to you are Spirit and Life!"*
(John 6:63 ESV)

*"For me, words are a form of action,
capable of influencing change."*
~Ingrid Bengi

1
Changing The Atmosphere

Being the one who makes the difference

"Once in a while it really hits people that they don't have to experience the world in the way they have been told to."
~Alan Keightley

"Most people grow old within a small circle of ideas that they have not discovered for themselves. There are, perhaps, less wrong-minded people than thoughtless."
~Marquis De Vauvenargues

Have you ever walked into a room and felt the atmosphere? There's an awareness somewhere deep inside you when people are cold or critical towards you and you don't feel welcome … or they've just been telling dirty jokes and sleaze is in the air … or when it's a warm, accepting environment.

Have you ever witnessed someone arrive in a certain place to see the atmosphere change immediately when they appear? Fear and control walked in with them, or fun and laughter that was infectious; everyone's mood changed when that one person turned up.

Have you ever been suddenly bombarded with thoughts of lust or despair or anger, without any outward reason? When that has happened, have you beaten yourself up over thinking that way? Or have you surrendered to and embraced those feelings? Have you considered whether there might be another reason why you are sometimes prey to thoughts you have not been inviting?

Have you ever visited places where great atrocities were committed, like the Killing Fields of Cambodia, Auschwitz concentration camp, or a massacre site in Rwanda? There's a horror embedded into every nook and cranny of those sites, no matter how sunny and peaceful they may be on the day of your visit. Conversely, have you been inside a great cathedral that has been envisioned and built by godly people? Somehow the atmosphere is saturated with the majesty and beauty of a holy God, combined with the reverence of generations of people who came there to pay Him homage.

There is an atmosphere over every place, every situation, and also every family, every nation – in fact, in every context in which people live, work and play. Guess what! That atmosphere was not there before the people arrived! It has been set by certain key people who have been given, or who have taken for themselves in the absence of anyone else doing it, the right and authority in the spiritual realm to establish that atmosphere. None of us live in a vacuum. But in the same way that a fish does not know what water is, mostly we take the atmosphere we inhabit for granted.

We may or may not like it, but more often than not we accept the atmosphere we live in as being normal. Even though we might be desperate to escape from it, we rarely understand that not only can we change it — it's our responsibility to change it. When a person is born again, a deposit of the Kingdom of God is placed into their lives. Christians are therefore commanded to carry the Kingdom of Heaven wherever the soles of our feet take us. When God's Kingdom comes in, anything that is not of the Kingdom has to give way. Wherever we go, we take His Kingdom with us (Luke 10:9-12).

Or at least, that's the ideal.

Often, people find themselves swamped by the toxic environment that surrounds them. Instead of changing it, it overwhelms and changes them.

When this happens, we easily lose perspective on our position as children of the living God, becoming so accustomed to the prevailing spiritual atmosphere that, after a while, we don't see anything wrong with it. We begin to find it easier and easier to join in with things that we once found uncomfortable and alien to our faith. The longer this persists, the more we blend in, so that we are no longer identifiable as being different. In time we become numb to the discomfort of the atmosphere as we harden our hearts to cope with it. By then, we have begun to make our own contribution to keeping the atmosphere as it is.

Either that, or we spend a good deal of our time praying or fretting about our environment and begging God to make something happen to change it — or simply to get us out of there! We don't realise that God already did something to change the atmosphere: He put us there! You and I are the ones with the spiritual authority in the places where we work or play or live. You don't have to be the General Manager of your company, the biggest wage earner in your house or the most popular person in a group to have spiritual authority in that situation. You could be a checkout chick or a student or a house-husband, but if you understand that Jesus Christ has delegated His authority to you, then you will know that you have the authority to set the atmosphere in the place you are in – be it a major corporation or a children's playgroup.

It's important to develop the skill to know the difference between allowing our behaviour to deteriorate, so that we fit into an atmosphere we once knew was not right, and realising that some of our religious stances are just that – religious. Some of the things we previously felt were ungodly, such as dancing or drinking alcohol or hanging out the washing on a Sunday, were merely religious laws put into place in order to legislate our behaviour.

Christianity can't be legislated. It has to be lived out of relationship. Jesus never said that we ought not to drink alcohol, but the Bible is full of warnings against getting drunk. Miriam danced, David danced, but so did Herod's step-daughter, Salome. Dancing is an age old exercise that God made us for, something He knew would give us joy. Having said that, pole dancing wasn't what He had in mind!

If we are in relationship with God and value His word above our own opinion and other peoples', we will not need a rulebook to keep us from falling into sin. We will naturally understand where to draw the line. The Amplified Bible puts it best:

"I will give you the keys of the Kingdom of Heaven; and whatever you bind (declare improper and unlawful) on earth must be what is already bound in heaven; and whatever you loose (declare lawful) on earth must be what is already loosed in heaven." (Matthew 16:19 Amp)

This translation makes it clear that in order to forbid or release aspects of God's heavenly atmosphere on earth, we must first understand from God the perspective of Heaven. That puts a totally different slant on it, doesn't it.

It's true that there are some situations where it's difficult for us to perceive what might be happening in Heaven, so it's best to begin with the easy things first. For instance, we know without a doubt that there's no pornography in heaven, so we have the right to take authority over the spiritual realm to forbid this in our household and our church. As we learn to do that, we can take it a step further and forbid it in our work place and then in our city. There's no tax dodging, no filthy language, no cruelty, no immorality, no lying, no greed, no gossip in Heaven ... get the picture?

It's a great place to start.

Just one warning though...

We need to make sure we deal with any issue in our own life before we try dealing with it in a larger context. If we don't make sure we're clean on the inside (Matthew 23:27), our enemy the devil will bide his time, waiting for the perfect moment when he can flatten us faster than we can turn around. So many times great role models have been exposed as hypocrites because of undealt with issues in their lives that eventually brought them down. An ignominious fate can befall anyone who neglects to sort themselves out before they go out to change the world. I discussed this at length in the first chapter of my previous book, *Catalysts: You Can Be God's Agent For Change.* Many great Christians have been seduced by the spiritual activity in the atmosphere around them and then been trapped by their own pride into trying to apply their God-given authority in some external situation, when they haven't conquered that same issue in their own life. It's been the ruination of them and the Body of Christ has suffered the loss of great warriors and leaders as a result.

So, how do we work to transform an ungodly atmosphere into one that displays the properties of the Kingdom of Heaven?

First, it's important to realise that it isn't about getting everyone saved. Obviously it would be great for that to happen, but wherever we are, our first task is to bring the Kingdom into our environment so that our world will be under its influence. That means taking our God-given responsibilities seriously, but it doesn't mean beginning every interaction with a short preach about how much Jesus loves the person we are speaking to.

So what does the Kingdom of God look like? Inherent in God's Kingdom are peace, strength and wisdom, innovation, purity, righteousness, joy and laughter and truth... the list is literally endless, because it is comprised of the attributes of God Himself.

The keys to the Kingdom that Jesus gave to us include the understanding that He has given us the mandate and authority to change our world. That can only take place context by context and atmosphere by atmosphere. As we bring change to the places where we live and work, whether that's a shop in the UK, an orphanage in Africa, a church in Jakarta or a major corporation in Canada, our world changes too. And as our world changes, so do the worlds of our colleagues and their families and friends. When we take the Kingdom wherever we go, the whole atmosphere changes.

Elijah understood this principle and took seriously his responsibility as a changer of atmospheres.

"Elijah was a man with a nature like ours, and he prayed fervently that it might not rain, and for three years and six months it did not rain on the earth." (James 5:17)

1 Kings 17-18 tells the story of Ahab, the most evil king of Israel up to that point. As often happens when a nation is in trouble, God raised up a voice for Himself from nowhere – in this case, Elijah the Tishbite. Septuagint says Tishbe means "of the settlers".

Remember, what you settle for is where you'll live.

Elijah rose up and out from a people who had settled for the way their society was. He wasn't content with that. Nor did he waste his time complaining about the status quo. He was intentional about changing it. He was determined to make the king aware that the nation was headed for destruction and this culminated in him commanding it not to rain on the land.

And the rain stopped...

...for three and a half years.

God hid Elijah during those years and despite Ahab's best efforts, he remained hidden until the right time. When God has a plan and you're a willing participant, there's nothing the enemy can do to abort it. Elijah's role was to discern the purposes of God for his society and to intentionally facilitate a change of atmosphere. He had to decide to engage with God's plan. He understood that making no decision would be, by default, making a decision. When we hesitate between two options and don't choose either, one is automatically chosen for us – and it's not usually the good one. God won't force us into His plan, but the enemy has no qualms about writing his agenda for our lives and our family and our nation.

That means that when we don't engage with God's atmosphere-changing plans, our decision (or lack of a decision) will determine our future.

Elijah challenged the spiritual climate by calling for a duel: he and his God versus the prophets and their gods. Elijah questioned the people who assembled to watch this competition as to why they were hesitating between the two different opinions about which god to serve. He laid down a challenge to the false prophets that each party would call on their own god. The one who answered by fire would show himself to be the genuine God. Elijah was not intimidated by the fact that there were hundreds in the opposing party. He knew that any one person plus God is a majority.

The prophets of Baal danced around their altar, cutting themselves and shrieking, but no one answered them. Elijah mocked their frenzy, suggesting that possibly their god was thinking or had gone to the toilet, or was away on holiday. When it was his turn, he took his time over building the altar of the Lord, unexpectedly digging a trench around it and pouring 12 jars of the drought stricken nation's most precious commodity, water, all over the sacrifice and the wood until it lay in the trenches, making the possibility of fire, impossible.

Elijah was able to pull this off because he had heard from God. He had seen Heaven's perspective and understood how committed God was to using him to change the atmosphere. We can't demonstrate that to others until we know it for ourselves. We can't help others to break through until we've encountered the God of the breakthrough ourselves. It takes commitment and effort to bring a change to the atmosphere in our school or home or business. It requires a decision and then a willingness on our part to carry the weight of that decision, despite the fact that the journey may be unpleasant, difficult and may cost us personally. It will be impossible to do unless we understand there is a purpose at stake that is bigger than our personal comfort levels. It's about knowing that God wants to use us to usher His Kingdom into our environment.

"Then God said, 'Let us make man in our image, according to our likeness; let them have dominion over the fish of the sea, over the birds of the air and over the cattle, over all the earth and over every creeping thing that creeps on the earth.'" (Genesis 1:26)

It was always God's intention that we rule our world. Adam and Eve had authority over the satanic forces that were intruding into Eden, but their authority didn't last long because they lacked a true awareness of it and they were deceived into giving it away. Before they got used to it, it was gone. For centuries mankind lived under the influence of enemy forces until the Saviour came. With the death and resurrection of Jesus, the right and responsibility of the dominion of humankind was restored – but this time under the delegated authority of Jesus.

"The seventy-two returned with joy, saying, 'Lord, even the demons are subject to us in your name!' And he said to them, 'I saw Satan fall like lightning from heaven. Behold, I have given you authority to tread on serpents and scorpions, and over all power of the enemy, and nothing shall hurt you. Nevertheless, do not rejoice in this, that the spirits are subject to you, but rejoice that your names are written in heaven.'" (Luke 10:17-21)

We don't live in a spiritual vacuum. In fact the spiritual realm is more real and intense than most of us experience in the natural realm. We've been so desensitised by the sin of many generations that we have lost our awareness that we are made in the image of

God and, like God, must speak our world into order. We do, in fact, create our environment through what we say – but so often we shape our world with negative words: what we are worried about, what's gone wrong, who we think is against us.

We judge ourselves by our intentions and everyone else by their actions.

If we don't set God's agenda into the atmosphere over a situation, then someone else will. And that person is unlikely to be using His Word to do it. In every situation there is a "will of God" to be enacted and an adversary to that will – and it's the adversary that we are up against in every case. It's never our partner or teacher or boss or church leader who is the problem. It is only ever our adversary, the devil, who uses situations and misunderstandings and people to discourage and demoralise us.

Setting the spiritual atmosphere in our own sphere of influence is our responsibility. If you are the only Christian in your workplace, it's your responsibility to set the atmosphere. If you're the only believer in your home, you can set the spiritual atmosphere. If you're the strongest believer in a given context (meaning that those around you are Christians, but the context itself isn't operating in a Christian way), realise that it's still your responsibility to bring in the Kingdom (Luke 10:8-12). The temptation is to believe that you're not strong enough, or you're too tired, or you shouldn't have to. But if you don't, who will? If two of you can see it, even better. Put aside your conflict, see beyond the pressure and pray in unity to establish what is happening in Heaven in your situation. This rarely involves addressing the issues publicly; it's about perceiving the situation and speaking out the things you know to be happening in Heaven, over that place. Literally, it's about Speaking Life – the language of God – into the atmosphere around you.

Whenever violence and ugliness occur in our world, it's as a result of the violence that is taking place in the spiritual realm. Whenever there's a mindless attack, when wars break out domestically or nationally, or a child is molested or a business goes under, or friends become enemies, it's because the violence in the spiritual realm has reached such extreme proportions that it breaks through into the natural world. By observing what's happening in our world, we can ascertain what is happening in the spiritual dimension.

* * *

Being in ministry means spending time with people who have problems. This can be a problem in itself if we are not aware of how to deal with it. When Rick and I were young in ministry, we would often spend hours talking people through issues in their marriage, only to come home and argue for three days. Gradually we realised that we were somehow picking up the issues that others were troubled by. So, when we came home from marriage counselling and began arguing ourselves over what seemed to be nothing, it was because we had "caught" something from the atmosphere that the people we were counselling had allowed themselves to be subjected to. Grasping this concept is far more difficult than dealing with it. Often we don't realise that an issue is not our own – we have merely been affected through our involvement in the situation.

Once we realised that our unexplained irritation stemmed from the spiritual realm over the marriage we were trying to help, we understood how to fix it. It wasn't actually our problem, and knowing that enabled us to deal with it quickly. One or both of us would stop focusing on our argument (sometimes a difficult thing to do when you're on a roll) and begin to take authority over the atmosphere that had smeared itself onto us, causing us to squabble over nothing. We addressed this by praying something similar to the words below. This isn't a mantra or a formula, just a guide to give you an idea:

"In the name of Jesus I take authority over the work of the enemy that comes to destroy the peace of our marriage. I break the power of this discord by the blood of Jesus Christ. In the name of Jesus, we refuse to be affected by the atmosphere we've been in and choose to place ourselves under the influence of Jesus Christ and Him only. Lord, you set the atmosphere for our marriage."

We were, and still are after all these years, amazed at the immediacy of the result. The argument was gone, the heat cooled and unity was restored. But it needed us to be aware that we were up against a spiritual influence that was not from God, and to refuse to be drawn into the rights and wrongs of our anger, choosing instead to lay down our so called rights to deal with spiritual issues in a Kingdom way.

Don't get me wrong. It doesn't mean that we don't disagree and argue at times; we surely do. We are two different people with different opinions and it makes sense that sometimes we have disagreements that need to be talked out. This is not about that. It's about knowing when something that is not of God has latched onto you in a way that prevents the Kingdom of God from being expressed through you – rather than being fooled into letting it stay because you think it's normal. There are many examples, but I'll give just one more.

Churches rely heavily on volunteer labour; they couldn't function without it. Some years ago we were in an office environment in which there were many volunteers, with and without titles. We had an office manager, let's call her Lucy, who did a great job of overseeing the general running of the offices, and we had a fantastic team who empowered the work of the church by their dedication and selflessness.

The office was generally a place of laughter and productivity. However, as often happens in any organisation, there was a fly in the ointment. We had one worker who seemed to always have an issue. Although generally a nice woman, she was often very difficult to get on with and one day the office manager came to me in distress, telling me that whenever this woman came into the office, she was often so unpleasant that many of the team of volunteers would go home rather than have to work in the same space as her.

The problem was getting out of hand as people increasingly found other things to do in preference to working with the lady in question. Lucy was at her wits end. We discussed the matter over a coffee and I told her about what Rick and I were discovering about taking authority over the atmosphere and commanding a godly environment. Lucy, as office manager in a team of Christians, could take authority over the atmosphere of our church office and bind every attitude in it that was not in Heaven, and loose over the office whatever was clearly the purpose of Heaven for the office and the team.

We decided to conduct an experiment. We would not tell anyone else about this, just the two of us would know, and I wouldn't pray about it; Lucy would be the only one to pray. Every morning, just for a few minutes, she prayed asking God what His will was for our office and church team. After that she would take authority over the attitudes causing problems in the office, breaking the spiritual powers of control, of pride and fear, of petty jealousy and spite and rejection and any other things that came to mind. She would call on the power of the blood of Jesus Christ to cleanse the office of those things and then command the things that were loosed in Heaven to be loosed in the office. These were such things as joy, laughter, efficiency, servanthood, grace, vision, etc.

Please note that she did not attempt to influence anyone's behaviour or role by saying what they should do, she only spoke over the atmosphere. We don't have authority over other people, but we do have authority over whether the atmosphere is godly or not. This is how people like Corrie Ten Boom could live and work and make such a difference in a concentration camp. She didn't change the guards or the prisoners, but as a godly and spiritually-aware person, working against the spiritual atmosphere in that camp, she and her sister changed the atmosphere over their own bunkhouse. Many others have done the same in their own situations.

We were both astonished at the results that came so quickly. The first thing that happened was that when this lady came into the office, the laughter and general wellbeing of the other workers wasn't abated. No one seemed to feel the need to walk on eggshells any more in order to avoid her ire. Within days, the lady in question began to come in later and go home earlier, then began to come less days in the week, until finally one day she announced that she would not be working in the church anymore as she could do with a rest and things weren't the same as they used to be. What she was saying, although she didn't know it, was that the atmosphere was no longer subject to her moods because now it was subject to the Kingdom of Heaven. This all happened within a few weeks and no one except Lucy and myself knew how Lucy had been praying.

Let me add this. The atmosphere changed to such a degree that the team member was no longer able to control it and left instead. However, had she been willing to be changed by the godly atmosphere that was at work in the place, there would have been no need for her to go. The others changed and were no longer intimidated by her bullying. She could have changed too, but unconsciously she preferred to leave rather than submit to the godly atmosphere that Lucy had set in place.

* * *

Ahab's leadership meant that the nation of Israel was going down the pan. It was the season for Heaven to come and help. On seeing the state of the nation, Elijah had proclaimed a drought that affected him as much as everyone else. No rain meant no food. But Elijah's faith grew during this period as God fed him first at the brook and then through the widow who didn't initially have enough to feed herself.

In an economic climate of Government cutbacks, unemployment and belt tightening, Elijah and the widow give us answers for ourselves. The Church is rising in Missio Dei. God's heart for His people is being expressed as many Christians rise to advance the Kingdom of God by fighting against trafficking, systemic poverty, AIDs, vulnerable children, homelessness, addictions...

...but where will the money come from?

Christian business people are being inspired and equipped to change their world by funding compassionate projects with innovative and entrepreneurial business ideas. In effect: Business with a Mission. The great apostolic church leader and businesswoman, Pat Francis of Kingdom Covenant Ministries near Toronto, says:

Charity sees the need and enterprise provides the solution.

This means that we cannot afford to allow our thinking to be subject to the prevailing economic climate, no matter how it may look. It's one thing to be aware of the situation, that makes sense, but it's another thing altogether to simply accept the situation as being unchangeable. Find out what's happening in Heaven and speak that life over your context on earth. Look to the Lord for promotions, new contracts, for more work, innovative ideas for business, even if you haven't been in business before. Believe for it! Don't accept the status quo. Don't allow the world's economy to dictate how much you can provide for the Kingdom projects that are on your heart.

God can provide water for the sacrifices you've made so that He can be *seen* as your God – just as He did for Elijah. He can supply not only your need, like He did for the prophet at the brook, but He also wants to miraculously use the little you have to provide for His purposes, as He did for the widow. Her faith in giving her almost non-existent portion meant that not only was the prophet provided for, so that he could do what God had called him to, but she and her son were provided for as well throughout that time of economic downturn. The story is as much about her faith as Elijah's.

Heaven isn't broke! There is provision for needs and wealth and resources to give birth to God's purposes, whatever your situation. Ask God what is in Heaven in regard to your spiritual, moral, financial, physical and emotional wellbeing. When you see it as God sees it, you can command the things that operate against you to be bound here as they are in Heaven, and the things that are loosed in Heaven to be loosed into your situation.

The drought was broken, but the work of bringing change was not. Elijah prayed for the impossible and spoke it out as words of life into the dryness around him, believing that the God who had called him thus far would be faithful to finish what He had started (1 Thessalonians 5:24). He knew God.

He had learned in faith that God would provide for him personally, so he was able to live at the next level of faith, that God would answer with fire in the face of the impossible as well as bring desperately needed rain to the nation. We have to learn to receive God's provision for ourselves before we learn to bring breakthrough to other people and nations, but this means stepping out and doing it, rather than protecting our own interests. We have to learn to see the little clouds and not dismiss them as "not enough", but to keep speaking the life of God over our needs and see every tiny encouragement as a sign of breakthrough.

"Arise, shine, for your light has come, and the glory of the Lord has risen upon you. For behold, darkness shall cover the earth and thick darkness the peoples; but the Lord will arise upon you, and his glory will be seen upon you. And nations shall come to your light, and kings to the brightness of your rising." (Isaiah 60:1-3)

That means us! When we were born again, Heaven was birthed in our hearts to enable us to be light in the darkness. We are carriers of the Kingdom and if that doesn't show up in our families, jobs, churches, businesses and finances, then it's not light in the darkness.

We may lose at times; we surely do, but don't accept that as being all there is to it! There are times when you're just sitting next to a dried up river and you're so broke and broken that if it weren't for the birds or the widows feeding you, you would starve. We all have times and seasons like that, but they do not last forever. Don't accept them as your lot in life!

Keep standing, knowing in your heart that God has called you to be someone who brings change to the atmosphere. He's not going to let you down, even if things are tough right now. Faith speaks out the life of Christ over what needs to happen for God's will to be done, so His Kingdom can come on earth as it is in Heaven.

Despite the miracle, the crisis wasn't over and Elijah knew that better than anyone. By faith he told Ahab that it was about to rain. The rain was there in the spiritual realm but it didn't exist on the earth yet. Ahab went off to eat, but Elijah climbed a mountain because the job wasn't finished. There was still work to be done to change the atmosphere over the nation and Elijah was determined to see it through.

Following through on our intention to change the atmosphere means we will continue to wait on God while everyone else gets on with normal life.

Elijah knew the rain would come and break the drought because God had shown him that at the beginning. We have to have heard from God in order to be able to see a situation through.

The servant watched him and learned. Observe people of faith; see what they do and how they do it. Presumption isn't faith – faith is about knowing the character of God to such a degree that if it's not God saying "no", you know you don't have to take "no" for an answer. Don't be changed by the atmosphere you're in; change it by your own intentional decision to bring God's Kingdom in! There is a will of God for that place. It's your task to command it to be so. If in Heaven your work place is to be peaceful, productive and prosperous, command it to be so on earth. It's a rare revelation to not take "no" for an answer, when we know it's not God who's saying no to a particular situation, but we can all ask for it. The Kingdom of God is built by such people, who see what needs to be changed and give their lives over to doing it. Whether it's in your family, your business, your mission or ministry ... wherever God has called you, usher in His Kingdom.

2
Getting
Perspective

The context for speaking life

"We don't see things as they are; we see them as we are."
~Anaïs Nin

"People who look through keyholes are apt to get the idea that most things are keyhole shaped."
~Author Unknown

Someone once said, perspective is everything. They were right!

Saul and his brave army were transformed in an instant from men of war into a bunch of snivelling, fearful cowards by the sight of the giant of doom parading in front of them. The Israelites were prepared to meet other soldiers like themselves, but this behemoth was something beyond anything they'd been trained to deal with. Every onlooker knew, without a shadow of doubt, that they were trapped and the only way out was to run. Fear drained their last drops of strength as Goliath strode back and forth on the opposite mountain each morning and evening, the rising and setting suns refracting off his bronze armour into their eyes, destroying their ability to see anything else but him. The sound of his voice crushed whatever courage they might have mustered as it rang across the valley like the roar of a lion, challenging and arrogant, daring them to fight...

...daring them to die.

The facts were in front of them ... and the facts were overwhelming.

And then there was David, fresh from the sheep fields and fresh from his own fears and fights. Unarmoured, unadmired, unnoticed, he had fought lions and bears, braving dangerous situations because of his father's belief that he could keep the sheep safe. Alone in the backside of the desert, David had learned all about perspective in a season and environment where there was no one to applaud, no one to comfort and no one to wipe the blood and sweat from his face.

Ironically, it was his fear that had taught him the early lessons of faith. He'd called out to his God as he ran in terror towards the lion that stalked the sheep and he was stunned and grateful to find that God answered him in spite of his fear. Or maybe because of it – because without fear there is no courage. As time went on and the battles increased, he had also increased, becoming more confident as he gained the understanding that regardless of the size of his enemy, his God was always bigger.

By the time David arrived at the battlefields, bringing the hamburgers to his brothers, he had learned about the value of perspective.

And then he found out that they hadn't. When the giant rocked up that afternoon something had changed, even though he didn't know that at the time, and nor did anyone else.

The unseen change was that David had a different perspective to everyone else on that battlefield, Israelite or Philistine. Most people predict the outcome of a battle based on the size of the protagonists. And that is a normal, natural, sensible thing to do – except where God is involved. When God's on your side, size really doesn't matter because God is bigger than any opposition anywhere in any context.

David had learned this.

The onlookers had not.

David observed the scene as it played out in front of him, but he had difficulty relating to the problem. Revelation from God gives supernatural insight, but we often mistakenly believe that other people understand the same things we do. Revelation comes when knowledge has made the long journey from your mind to your understanding and suddenly becomes real to you. When you have revelation of a spiritual concept you can live by it and die for it – but don't expect other people to grasp it or agree. David's eldest brother Eliab certainly didn't, accusing him of being an attention seeker, as older siblings have a tendency to do.

Faith can look like arrogance to people who don't have it, but David was in the process of changing the atmosphere over the battlefield.

Revelation is a personal thing. People who haven't gained revelation of the way God's word can change any situation often misunderstand the concept of speaking life. David's revelation enabled him to view Goliath from God's perspective, and the fact that he was the little brother, younger and shorter than everyone else in his family, wasn't relevant. The fact that the giant's armour was heavier than the average man didn't faze him either. It wasn't about how Goliath looked in comparison to David, it was about what he looked like in comparison to God. David was looking with God's eyes, so he didn't see a living nightmare.

All he saw was an overgrown, uncircumcised Philistine.

It's always about perspective.

Goliath, still not perceiving the turn of the tide, came clad in all his weaponry. He was partly amused but mostly affronted at the sight of the boy who'd been sent to fight him.

The perception of the home team hadn't changed either. Their fear intensified as they watched the encounter, expecting a predictable end to an unpredictable confrontation. Their greatest fear was for themselves, because this confrontation, no matter how obvious its conclusion, would precipitate all-out war and they were in no doubt as to their fate. Only David understood that the course of the battle had changed irrevocably. He ran toward the giant, calling out as he went – not in prayer, but with a declaration of God's perspective.

"Then David said to the Philistine, 'You come to me with a sword and with a spear and with a javelin, but I come to you in the name of the Lord of hosts, the God of the armies of Israel, whom you have defied. This day, the Lord will deliver you into my hand and I will strike you down and cut off your head. And I will give the dead bodies of the host of the Philistines this day to the birds of the air and the wild beasts of the earth, that all the earth may know that there is a God in Israel and that all this assembly may know that

*the Lord saves not with sword and spear. For the battle is the Lord's
and He will give you into our hand.' When the Philistine arose and
came and drew near to meet David, David ran quickly toward the
battle line to meet the Philistine. And David put his hand in his bag
and took out a stone and slung it and struck the Philistine on his
forehead. The stone sank into his forehead and he fell on his face to
the ground. So David prevailed over the Philistine with a sling and
with a stone, and struck the Philistine and killed him. There was no
sword in the hand of David."* (1 Samuel 17:45-50 ESV)

A different perspective speaks a different language. David's words
sounded like bravado, arrogance, lunacy, to the people who stood
watching and listening, but David's different perspective meant
that he spoke a different language.

As it turned out, David was speaking the language of life and it had
the effect of altering the atmosphere and causing a paradigm shift
there in that place where fear had previously reigned.

Speaking life is a natural result of having God's perspective and
David knew how to speak life. He had begun practicing it in the
sheep fields when fear threatened to overwhelm him. He'd been
practicing it when feelings of total irrelevance to his family and to
the state of the nation of Israel threatened to engulf his vision and
destiny. He continued to practice it when all the evidence pointed
to the fact that he was doomed to a life of insignificance, working
forever in the backblocks as a shepherd. The language he spoke
came out of his understanding of God's nature and perspective.
How he saw and how he spoke were connected. In seeing what
God saw, he was able to say what God said. God speaks life. Always!
David's revelation changed an atmosphere where bullying and fear
were the norm for the Israelite warriors, to one of courage and
victory.

One of the most encouraging things about following Jesus is that He makes sense. There's freedom in listening to what He says and letting it change the way we do things.

The language Jesus speaks is the language of life. The apostle John says that *life* was in Jesus, and that *life* was the *light* of mankind. In this context, life and light are one and the same. Literally, His life shines out the light of revelation, and revelation is synonymous with spiritual understanding.

Spiritual understanding is what enables us to follow through on the task ahead because spiritual awareness means our hearts are engaged, not just our minds. Learning to speak Jesus' language is not an easy task, especially for jaded 21st century post moderns whose cynical perspective comes from having seen it all, done a lot of it, and who are very tired and disillusioned with their worn out, logo'd t-shirts. Revolving fads, when combined with the general cynicism that is infused into the very air we breathe, can make the language of life seem like just another trend. However, speaking life isn't merely positive speaking, nor is it some *name it and claim it* brand of fake faith which often masks a tendency to live in denial. Speaking life relates to the deepest parts of who we are and how our hearts communicate – with the world, with each other, and with God.

Life has always been God's language, spoken even before life on earth began. The first time we hear it spoken is at the time of creation. Genesis 1:2 says that the earth was, "without form" (*tohu*), it was "void" (*bohu*) and that "darkness covered the face of the deep". At that point the earth was nothing but a shapeless, confused wasteland set in a vacuum of darkness. And then God spoke.

It's interesting to note that God didn't actually do anything. There was no flurry of activity beforehand; no angels flying in with startling messages as we see in other important events, like the birth of Jesus. In the beginning, God started with what He had, which was literally nothing but confusion, waste and darkness, and then He added a few words to the mixture. They were small, simple words, but they made all the difference.

Why? *They were words of life!*

"And God said, 'let there be light,' and there was light." (Genesis 1:3)

Without any fuss or grandstanding, God dealt with the darkness of this chaotic empty world. With just a few words of life, everything changed. The light went on, even though at that point there was no sun, no moon or stars. There was absolutely nothing to create light, but light, as an entity of its own, appeared, and from that point the scene was transformed. The light poured out of the life He spoke.

Light has a way of changing everything. Sometimes it feels like we're totally in the dark, confused and lost. We lack direction and the capacity to clearly see our position, so our circumstances easily trip us up. But when light comes, we can begin to see how to go from where we are.

God can work as well in the dark as in the light (Psalm 77:2). It's all the same to Him. But He knows that we need to see what's going on. That's why His first step in the process of transforming emptiness and chaos, whether on the planet or in our personal world, is to give light. Light brings understanding and revelation. The dictionary defines revelation as "valuable information that is newly disclosed." Literally, when the light turns on, we find valuable information that we didn't see before. Once He had brought light, progress was rapid in God's creation program as He continued to speak divine order into the world.

* * *

The Bible says that we have been formed in the image of God (Genesis 1:27). That doesn't mean that physically we have the same amount of hands and feet, fingers and toes as Him, or the same eyes, nose and mouth. The similarity between Him and us is not physical, but based on the fact that He is a spiritual being and so are we. Physiologically, we can say that we are a spirit, we own our soul and we live in our body. This is why racism is so profoundly and utterly ludicrous. Our God is not brown, black or white. He's not Asian, Caucasian or Negroid. He is Spirit and that is the image we carry. Regardless of our physical attributes, in our deepest place of "self-ness", we are a spirit, made in the image of our God who is Himself Spirit.

All animals have a body and soul, but only human beings have a spirit. When God breathed life into humanity on that new day, it was Adam's spirit that became alive, and as a consequence, his soul and his body lived also.

Humans are the only beings on earth that can communicate with God directly – spirit to Spirit. The fact that we are spiritual beings is what makes us like God, which is why we will live eternally in whatever destination our choices decide for us. In reality, the person we are (spirit and soul, inextricably linked) cannot die. That is why it's so important that we are in relationship with Jesus Christ who died and rose again so that we could live with our Father God in Heaven, the place he designed for us to live eternally. That eternal part of us, our spirit, is the aspect that relates directly with God, person-to-person, heart to heart, quite literally spirit-to-spirit.

Our soul comprises our mind, will and emotions, which takes into account talent, personality, likes and dislikes. It's the part of us that makes us identifiable as who we are and determines the things that we identify with. It's the part of us that loves rock music or rock climbing or rock gardens, hip hop or Beethoven, surfing the net or surfing the waves, making home made beer or home making or building houses or reading or playing board games or playing extreme sports.

The soul and spirit are inextricably linked and will go together to Heaven when our body finally gives up – the only part of our "self" that is dispensable. Like the other aspects of ourselves, our body grows and develops, but unlike the other parts, it also wears out and eventually stops functioning.

* * *

When God spoke into the dark chaotic waste, a brave new world began to form and it was literally built from the words He said.

"By faith we understand that the entire universe was formed at God's command, that what we now see did not come from anything that can be seen." (Hebrews 11:3)

Another translation says, "The worlds were prepared by the word of God so that what is seen is not made out of things that are visible."

That's a pretty heavy concept for us to understand, but it literally means that God had a vision and He spoke His vision into being. His language is life and He used words as the medium through which to call into being the things He had planned for the purpose He had in mind.

Literally, His words created the reality of what He was thinking. It's hard to believe at first, but because we are spiritual beings just like God, our language also has great spiritual impact, regardless of whether we believe in Him or not. Because we are created in His image, we share His capacity to frame and construct our own worlds with the words we speak.

And this works in every aspect of our language, whether negative or positive.

Speaking life is one of the most significant values of CGI, the church-planting organisation Rick and I founded in the UK in the late 1990s. As we worked to take our place in co-labouring with God to establish His Kingdom, we realised there was a vast difference between how events and situations appear to us, and how they appear to Him. We wasted a lot of time stressing as we faced off with giants that God was dealing with through us.

If we'd understood that earlier we would have got more sleep.

It was in the times we were afraid and yet, like David, still determined to deal with our personal lions and bears in the name of Jesus, that we gradually began to realise that God was seriously working with us to help us change the atmosphere. We began to understand that He was personally resident in the tiny, seemingly irrelevant little slingshots that we used in our battles against the giant problems and circumstances we often felt were arrayed against us.

Speaking life isn't denial. Situations are what they are and denying the facts and burying your head in the sand hoping that if you can't see them they won't be there, doesn't help anyone. In fact, catastrophe lies down that course of inaction. David didn't say that Goliath wasn't a giant. It was clear that he was. What he did was to challenge the giant's defiance as he mocked the armies of the living God. The reason he could do that was because he had gained confidence in the God whose perspective he had acquired in earlier, less public battles. It wasn't that he didn't see the problem clearly, but speaking life entails seeing the problem and then going beyond that to prophetically see and then say the solution in such a way as to change the atmosphere.

Literally, the art of speaking life is most clearly and effectively expressed as the believer looks at the evidence in front of him, acknowledging the reality of it, and then asks God for His perspective and begins to prophesy what God sees rather than what he sees. Once a person has God's perspective, they are able to move forward despite the natural fears that want to rise up to rob them of their strength and focus. This always requires choices, because the only person who can control what your tongue says, is you!

A similar scenario was played out when Elisha and his servant were faced with an army determined to take them prisoner (2 Kings 6:17). When the panic-stricken servant questioned his mentor's cool response to the danger they were in, Elisha prayed that his eyes would be opened so that he could see beyond the problem and into the solution.

The servant's deeper look, that prophetic second viewpoint, showed him God's perspective. An army of fire surrounded them; there were angels on every side. Supernatural rescuers had been sent by Heaven to overrule the plans of the enemy. The key was in Elisha seeing it, which is what enabled him to make the decision as to how to deal with it. He'd already been changing the atmosphere before this happened, so fear, when it arrived, found no place to settle.

Followers of Jesus must take the time to get God's perspective and learn the language that Jesus speaks. That way, the courage and capacity to follow through on what He has said to us will come naturally. Prophetic understanding rises out of relationship with God, igniting a desire to see beyond the natural realm and into the spiritual dimension

3
The Command
To Speak Life

...from a NO WAY position

"Have the courage to live. Anyone can die."
~Robert Cody

*"To have something you've never had before, you've got to
do something you've never done before!"*
~Unknown

When Rick and I first moved to the UK to work with what became Christian Growth International, God gave us a few strategic principles to inculcate into the nation we were called to. One of them was to develop a culture and atmosphere of speaking life into a people who were more used to focusing on the negatives of a situation than its possibilities.

In the months before we moved from Australia, the Lord spoke first to Rick and then to me from Ezekiel 37:1-10. God had transported Ezekiel into a hot, deserted valley filled with very dry bones. Because Ezekiel was reasonably used to God doing strange things with him, he waited to see what God would do.

But God didn't do anything. In fact, He focused on Ezekiel as though Ezekiel should be the one to make a move. He asked him a strange question: "Ezekiel, do you think these bones can live again?" Ezekiel, like anyone with any sense, understood that when God asks a question, it's not because He needs information.

"You know the answer to that, Lord."

* * *

Faith is confusing, especially because there are so many conflicting opinions about it, both in and outside of the Church. The tendency of most people is to confine faith to something small enough to cope with, while still being big enough to live in. For many people, faith functions like someone who owns a magnificent mansion but only lives in two small rooms downstairs at the front, never exploring or developing the rest of the house. Often we confine our faith to "I believe in Jesus" and beyond that maybe we can get to a place where we can believe God to provide enough for us to live on or help us get out of trouble.

More often than not, we don't pray about certain issues because we've already decided why and how God can't answer what we need. I can't count the number of times I've offered to pray with someone, after listening to their dilemma, only to be bombarded by a litany of reasons why God just couldn't help with *this* situation. Apparently, it was definitely beyond His capacity to think up anything that couldn't be stymied by the reasons listed by the person with the problem. We make God small enough to keep in our pockets, ready to ask for things we can believe for, but not large enough to actually help us when the chips are down and only miracles can save the day.

Faith is so much more than hoping and believing that we can pay our bills, keep our job and have our needs met.

* * *

Experiencing the dry bones in the valley confronted Ezekiel with his own lack of understanding of what God means when He speaks about possibilities. His decision to wait and see what God was getting at was a good one. Making the choice not to second-guess God presented Ezekiel with an opportunity to not only be an eyewitness to an amazing event, but also take his own part in it.

Speaking life is not denial.

God took Ezekiel on that stroll through Death Valley to show him how hopeless the situation was. The whole region was strewn with bones and they were very dry. The further they walked and the hotter the sun beat down on Ezekiel's head, the more sure he became of the facts laid out in front of him. There was obviously no hope for the inhabitants of this valley.

The only life forms present were God and Ezekiel. They were both aware of what they were looking at, and neither of them attempted to suggest anything other than that they were surrounded by very, very dry bones. Even the extreme heat of the desert air they breathed contained death. There was no life left in that arid atmosphere. And then God popped the question and Ezekiel bit his lip, desperate to stop himself from stating the bloomin' obvious. God wasn't asking Ezekiel to bury his head in the sand. He wasn't requiring him to deny the death that lay strewn all around them on the valley floor. He was giving Ezekiel first hand experience in living the truth that beyond impossibilities lie all the possibilities of His word. The God's-eye view is so different from anything we can perceive without His input. Remember how tightly Jericho was shut up and yet God told Joshua to see that He had given Him the city? God's perspective is always deeper, broader, longer and truer than anything our own eyes can see.

The facts say one thing, but the truths of God say something altogether different.

Putting the ball back into God's court, Ezekiel waited with bated breath to see what would happen next. It never occurred to him that the answer lay within him! He knew impossibility when he saw it and he also knew that God can make a way where there is no way.

Oddly enough, God doesn't seem to know the word "impossible". It's a word that doesn't translate into the language of life.
So God told Ezekiel to prophesy into the very arena of death and command life to reign there!

* * *

As we prepared to come to the UK, not knowing what was ahead of us or what kind of people we would be working with, God spoke to Rick from the story of the dry bone, saying: If you don't speak life into the place you are in ...you will become like the place you're in. We knew He meant that despite the fact that He'd deliberately planted us in this nation for the purpose of bringing life and change to that which was dead and dry, it was also possible for us to die in the location He'd placed us in, and our own disillusioned and disappointed bones would be added to the multitude of skeletons of destroyed hopers and dreamers that already lay there.

Or we could choose to play our part in changing our region and the nation by speaking life.

How often we rail at the circumstances we find ourselves in, without any comprehension that God has seeded us into that place because it needs a strong Christian presence. Our complaints and confusion give no credence to the thought that God might want us there so that the place can be changed, and the reason we are there is to facilitate that change.

It's easy to be overwhelmed with the seasons of our lives. Our businesses, ministries, families, jobs, marriages, finances, neighbourhoods, whatever our circles of influence, can sometimes feel like Death Valley. The arid, sandy desert soil is strewn with the bones of loss – broken dreams, old hopes, damaged relationships. Everything around us seems to lack anything of worth or value.

That may be so. The facts speak for themselves.

And yet the God who made us in His image, endowing us with His own attributes, spoke the universe into being (Hebrews 11:3). He fashioned an astonishingly beautiful and complex world out of the rawest of materials – chaos and waste – and His words of life. The success He experienced with this challenges us, as His people, about how we view the places He has carried us to, placed us in, and seeded our lives to grow into, in order that our lives can transform atmospheres in the same way His did. Whatever our view, He has another view. He asks us the same direct question He asked Ezekiel.

Can these bones, these places of brokenness and devastation, the lives and hopes that have been given over to death, live again?

It's at this point that we have to hold fast to remember that we are spiritual beings, just like Him, and our language, whether it be life or death, has great spiritual impact to bring change to the arena we've been placed into. Being created in His image means we have the capacity to frame our own worlds.

Hard to believe, isn't it? We're surrounded by death, just like Ezekiel. There's that bony skeleton of a marriage, children who are walking away from values that are dear to us, too many bills and too little money to pay them; we have hopes and dreams that seemed to be from God and yet, as the years go by, there is less and less reason or proof to validate their existence.

Can these bones live? You know, Lord.

* * *

And God commanded Ezekiel to prophesy, literally, to speak life into the death and destruction of that place, emulating in micro form what God Himself had done at the creation of the world out of the waste and chaos that was there. God told him what to say and Ezekiel said it, but even as he spoke, he didn't really believe it.

Well, perhaps that's not right. Let's say he knew that what he was called to say was impossible, but he also knew that God had commanded him to do it, so he suspended his disbelief and did what he was told. Sometimes faith is more about suspending our disbelief and going with what God says, despite what reason screams at us, than it is to do with any powerful sense of confidence.

So Ezekiel, feeling very glad that there was no one else around to witness him talking like a idiot, commanded life into the place of death and destruction, of waste, void and oblivion.

The operation of miracles is rarely as smooth or harmonious as we would expect. It's hard to imagine what happened next, because it was crazy, bizarre, the worst kind of nightmare. Ezekiel jumped back involuntarily as the bones began to rock violently and then leap from the sand in every direction. Erratic, clunking movements became more ordered as bone joined to bone. The rattling and clattering rose, becoming louder and louder until Ezekiel's ears were assaulted with a cacophony of raw, unrestrained noise.

Finally the clamour died away, to be replaced with a soft, slurping sound. He watched in horrified fascination as sinews, muscles and tendons began to form on the inert skeletons. His mind performed mental gymnastics in an attempt to understand what he was looking at. While he watched the scene changed again as skin began to form swiftly and silently on the raw red surface of the bodies on the ground.

Without warning, instead of being surrounded by bones, Ezekiel was surrounded by bodies.

Freaky!

And then... Everything got worse! Or better!

God, who'd been watching this without any expression on His face, turned and spoke to Ezekiel a second time.

"Ezekiel, restoration of these bodies is not enough. They need life. Speak to the breath and direct it to come into their lungs. Call it out from the four winds and command it to come and breathe into these bodies, so that they will live."

Ezekiel felt a lot less foolish now.

Awestruck! Overwhelmed! Astonished! But no longer foolish. He stood a little taller; his head somewhat higher than it was before, as confidence in the supernatural power of God operating in his life began to rise. He issued a bold command into the atmosphere.

He spoke life ... and life responded.

Suddenly, out of the still and silent heat, the desert was filled with wind. Sand flew into his mouth and nostrils; his hair blew in every direction as The Breath came roaring across the valley in obedience to God's command in Ezekiel's mouth, to be life to that which had no life.

Forcing its way into the nostrils of the mute, waiting bodies, their lungs were filled with The Breath. Eyes opened, arms and legs responded to the instructions of the now living brains and as Ezekiel watched...

An exceedingly great army stood to their feet. They stood to attention. They stood ready for battle. It didn't happen the way Ezekiel thought it would have happened... If he'd ever thought it could have happened.

Which he hadn't.

4
So What
Is Faith?

And how does it work?

> *"When you have come to the edge of all light that you know
> and you are about to drop off into the darkness of the unknown,
> Faith is knowing that one of two things will happen, there will be
> something solid to stand on ... or you will be taught to fly."*
> ~Patrick Overton

> *"You block your dreams when you allow your fear
> to grow bigger than your faith."*
> ~Mary Manin Morrisey

Faith is one of the most misunderstood, mislabelled and mismanaged elements of the Christian walk. There are so many attitudes and actions that masquerade as faith. People often base their life decisions on greed, ambition, naivety, risk or foolishness and they call it faith, and they think it is faith, which is why so many people end up disillusioned and burned out on fake faith or presumption. The problem is that if God doesn't tell you to do it, then taking risks is a stupid thing to do.

Conversely, if He does tell you to do it, you'd be a fool not to.

It's amazing how often God gets the blame when people make decisions without hearing from Him or despite hearing from Him, and it doesn't work. They get bitter and twisted with Him, and yet He wasn't invited into the decision making process in the first place or He was ignored when what He was saying didn't suit.

It's not faith unless God actually told you to do it. If He did, it will work, provided you stay focused and don't give up.

Some people live in such a way that it's clear to everyone who's sharing their world that what they say they believe isn't what they *actually* believe. They say one thing, but do something completely different. That leaves their brand of faith looking a lot like hypocrisy. Saying it and doing it are always two separate things. People can be fooled into thinking that because someone can recite faith statements off by heart, they must be living them. My husband says that you can tell what a person really believes by watching what they do, rather than listening to what they say.

You're not doing it unless you're doing it.

The book of Hebrews focuses a lot on faith – what it is, why it's necessary, the actions and behaviour of the people who have it, and what it accomplishes.

"Now faith is the assurance of things hoped for, the conviction of things not seen." (Hebrews 11:1)

In plain language, faith is absolutely confident that what it hopes for will come to pass, despite the fact that there's no way it could. What's required of us in faith is always bigger than what is possible.

That's a mouthful ... and one that a lot of people, even preachers, can easily choke on.

The passage in Hebrews goes on to talk about the people who are examples of faith, saying that it was their faith that caused them to gain approval. The whole chapter deals with people who made the choice to speak life into areas of huge doubt and impossibility because God told them to, and who received in the natural realm what had been brought to life in the spiritual realm...

...by their words.

Having begun to learn the language of life in the small, hidden, insignificant areas of their lives, where no one was the slightest bit interested in who they were or what they thought, they kept practicing until they'd developed the ability to speak it fluently.

Because if you can speak it at home ... you can speak it anywhere.

It takes a while to learn to speak a new language, and even longer to be able to think in it, but many ex-pats say that ultimately their learned, second language becomes their primary language. They now think in that language, which is why their speech becomes so fluent, regardless of their native language.

Learning to speak the language of life will work hugely in your favour and your life will be changed. Speaking life literally changes your present, which changes your future. It can even change the toxic effects of your past.

Speaking life is strategic to your ability to live your life in fullness. God spoke life and the world was created and we create our own worlds too as we speak life into our spheres of influence – home, neighbours, family, finance, work, church, ministry. Whatever aspect of life concerns us, we have the right to speak into it.

"And without faith it is impossible to please Him, for whoever would draw near to God must believe that He exists and that He rewards those who seek after Him." (Hebrews 11:6)

We have the power to change the world we live in if we grasp this concept. God appreciates our hard work, but hard work alone is tremendously wearing and often doesn't work. Without faith to give it the energy it needs, work alone will be debilitating and stressful. Duty without the joy that faith brings is a sad and thankless task. Watching dutiful, joyless Christians go about their daily chores is one of the major reasons why we've seen such a mass exodus of people from the Church over the last few decades and why so many facets of the Church experience only impotence. Faith on automatic pilot does that.

Loss of active faith breeds a lack of any kind of faith.

Who wants to spend their life in drudgery and powerlessness? Nobody that I know!

The trouble with a lot of Christians is that they have been trained to think that the joy of the Lord is a serious business. If we enjoy it, we're doing something wrong. Yet He's the One who gives righteousness, peace and joy in the Holy Ghost (Romans 4:17).

The Church is in the world to make a difference, bring change, and be the presence of Jesus Christ in the towns and cities we inhabit.

We literally have the power to change the atmosphere of the places we live in, but so often we don't even let ourselves go there in our minds and our prayers, just in case it doesn't work.

We've already persuaded ourselves that it won't.

Why pray when you're already convinced of all the reasons why what you're asking for can't happen? This is the default position of so many Christians who already know the reasons why God can't do anything to help them. Their spouse is too set in their ways, their job is going down, the finances are in a mess ... all things too hard for God to sort out and perform miracles in. These people have already settled on the reasons why nothing can change their situation and though they really love God, they do not attribute miracle-working power to Him. They already know why He can't do what they need, so they don't see the point in discussing it with Him and settle for life accompanied by a sub-standard version of faith – the impotence of which causes disillusionment to increase in them and those around them.

Remember, what you settle for is what you will live in.

The truth is that Christ followers have been deliberately seeded into nations, work places, communities, prisons, schools and other spheres of influence in order to change them. You're part of the culture you're in so that you can meet needs there AND change the atmosphere over your region.

That includes your own personal situations.

It's fine to have our own needs met. In fact, it's necessary because we learn the skills of faith by practicing how to wield words of life in our own lives. We grow our faith by practicing on ourselves and our circumstance. No one can help someone else break through in faith for finances until they know what it is to stand in faith to get their own bills paid. We can't assure someone that God will help their marriage unless we've experienced Him helping ours. We can offer others help because we stood and believed against all the odds that He could heal the wounds and bring wholeness to the fractures.

A very real aspect of our reluctance to do this is the fear of disappointment, because we don't realise that faith has to be learned and practiced. In the same way as we learn maths, beginning with simple addition and progressing through to multiplication and into fractions and increasingly complex equations, we learn how to walk in faith by beginning with simple problems and progressing from there as we work them out ... by faith.

We learn as much from our mistakes and failures as we do from our successes, if we're willing to keep working at it. Although in the subject of maths we may get frustrated at ourselves, we don't tend to take our failure personally. In our struggles to work out faith challenges, however, our default is often to be down on ourselves for lacking faith or, worse still, we become offended with God, reasoning that He is disinterested at best or, at worst, rejecting us personally.

Because we've learned from other Christians that God does answer prayer and is willing to help us with whatever we're going through, it's easy to lose the heart to pray when He doesn't seem to be doing that for us. We get offended with God's seeming lack of inclination to help us when the baby won't stop crying or the bills and the bank balance don't add up. We have a few practice runs at believing God, standing in faith, speaking life over our situation ... but, as happens with maths, we don't seem to get the right answers.

The temptation for many Christians (because we all suffer from a measure of rejection that stems back to the Garden of Eden) is to give up at this point. Christians so easily become jaundiced, embittered, offended by God, while still retaining a measure of love and belief in Him, and fall foul of the great temptation to settle back and live in a pale, stale, frail version of Christianity that has a form of godliness but denies its power (2 Timothy 3:5).

When we practice speaking life over our own circumstances, despite all evidence to the contrary, and learn to take the knocks and keep going until we gradually learn the principles of faith to see our prayers produce fruit, we develop the credibility and authority to speak life into someone else's circumstances. It's then that we can teach them to do the same. When people see the fruitfulness of a life of faith, complete with its failures as well as its successes, they gain strength and confidence that they may also be able to live like that.

The key is to not be afraid of failure, but to see it as a part of the process of learning to speak life and see breakthrough. Don't let fear of disappointment stop you from putting in the effort and energy to learn how to do it. Like riding a bicycle, there'll be a number of falls before you get a real handle on it (speaking from a good deal of personal experience, having learned to ride a bike as an adult!) It's easier to give up, but the exhilaration of grasping the rudiments and then the finer points of living a life of faith, is totally worth all the knocks and grazes and breaks.

* * *

One of the most commonly misunderstood aspects of faith is that we should be able to see the evidence of the thing we're in faith for. But that doesn't make sense.

It's not faith if it's already visible. Abraham is the perfect example. God had told him he would be the father of many nations...

...when he had no children at all.

Then God instructed him to change his name from Abram (meaning "father", which was already laughable enough under the circumstances), to Abraham (which means "father of multitudes"). In doing so, Abraham was speaking life in its most extreme form. Imagine the mocking that went on behind his back as he made the choice to call himself something that everyone knew he didn't have the ability to pull off.

His life so far was proof of his infertility.

But from that point on, because of his obedience, every time he spoke his own name and every time anyone else said it, they were speaking life into the infertility. It took years, but the strategy worked.

Joseph was in the same position. God gave him great dreams of leadership, the road to which was a couple of decades of slavery and prison combined with betrayal, temptation, false accusation and being forgotten, before he arrived at the fulfilment of those dreams. Yet he never gave up. He was a life speaker in every sense of the word, believing all the time that God would do what He said He would do, despite all evidence to the contrary. His trials were necessary to give him the maturity he would need for the leadership God had called him to.

Trials are great, because they give us the opportunity to be refined and strengthened, becoming more focused on what we're called to. They also allow us the freedom to break down and give up, which is what a lot of Christians decide to do. Having faith for the negative is incredibly destructive. Fear is...negative faith.

Many times people have more faith in what the devil can do than in what God can do.

The devil's version of faith is a rip-off of God's word. Taking scripture and twisting it like a knife into our hearts, he rewrites Hebrews 11:1 to read: "now fear is the substance of things dreaded, and the evidence of things not seen."

Our status as spiritual beings means that we, like God, have the capacity to speak into existence the things we are believing for, and then see those things come to pass.

Our conversation shows that some of us, without realising it, are standing in faith for all the worst things. We believe for catastrophe, for the negative, for difficulties and failures and the loss of our dreams, and as we speak our fear and failure out over and over again, we see those things come to pass. Job had it right when he moaned that what he had feared most had come upon him.

Check out your conversation. How positive is it? How heavily does it rely on the belief that God will provide all your needs and that He is able to do exceedingly abundantly above all that you could possibly ask or think? How much of the God-kind of faith do your words contain, and how much of the enemy's kind of faith do you habitually speak out?

At your place of work, do you fall in with the snide remarks and complaints others make about your colleagues? Or moan about your work load? Or undermine your boss? What would happen if you began to speak life into those situations and speak well of your family, your work, your church and the people who fill your world? What would you want to see at your work place? How about experimenting with the language of life?

Think about what God's perspective may be of your job, your boss, your marriage, your family, your financial needs, and then begin to thank God for it. Don't be put off by the enemy's knee jerk reaction as he fearfully attempts to make you think that what you are doing will never work. Just keep going!

Don't give up speaking life just because you're the only one doing it at the moment.

Don't give up speaking life because you're afraid that it sounds stupid.

Don't give up speaking life because someone else told you to be realistic.

Stop complaining, stop being afraid, stop automatically leaning towards the most negative option possible, and begin to speak life into your relationships and your needs and hopes, and see what will happen. Remember, the criterion for faith is that it has to be not happening in order for faith to come into play.

We live in such finite, cramped little worlds where we allow ourselves to think that there's no hope because what we want isn't happening. But if that is the truth, then our hope can be in God. He is the only way these things can change. If we cut Him off at the pass by saying, "There's no point, it will never work," we will get what we are standing in faith for. It won't work. There won't be any point. We'll have what we spoke into being.

Sometimes we try and fail and we don't try again, but the Bible says people are known by their fruit, not their individual successes. Fruit is borne slowly, over a period of time. You'll have successes and you'll have failures – we all do and that's life – but the fruit of a life that speaks the language of life is an abundance of life, despite the ups and downs that come to all of us.

This is the difference between the people who see miracles and the people who don't. The world has a survival mentality that is based on the negative. Its mantra is, "Don't hope and you won't be disappointed."

The Kingdom of Heaven has a different philosophy, a philosophy that requires the belief that the God who runs the universe is interested in me and He has a plan for my life; that the things I'm gifted at and passionate about are there because they fit into the plan. It's a plan that requires our cooperation. We need to believe there is a plan and that we don't have these passions for nothing. Then we make a decision to cooperate with God to see that plan come to pass.

"...so you see, it is impossible to please God without faith. Anyone who wants to come to Him must believe that there is a God and that He rewards those who diligently seek Him." (Hebrews 11:6)

It's reasonably easy to get the first bit right. We come to Him because we believe that there is a God, but we often don't take into account that there is a reward for people who keep seeking Him in a focused way after they've found Him, whether they've failed or been disappointed or suffered great loss.

Keep learning new things about God and about faith. Don't go down the road towards Him and then stall at the lights. When God is saying GO and it's all there ahead of you, don't let fear grip you and keep you from speaking life into the way ahead.

* * *

When God began to speak to Rick and I and the CGI team about Cherish (www.cherishuganda.org), our project for orphaned children suffering from HIV/AIDs in Uganda, we had absolutely nothing. No money, no property, no experience with missions or Africa or AIDs, no understanding even of what was required. But God put a vision in our hearts and we made the choice to go for it, knowing that if it failed, it would come down with a mighty crash, but also knowing that it was His vision and we could trust Him to see us through it.

How did we know that? Through experiencing the sound of His guidance at other times.

After a while, you get to know the sound of His voice, if you stay humble and courageous and obedient and provided you keep listening. People who have been in love for many years can pick up their partner's voice even in a crowd, even at a party, because of the years of their intimacy, of having the sound of each other's voice so deeply ingrained in their psyche that other sounds can't drown it out. In the same way, the more time you spend relating to God about everything that pertains to you, the clearer His voice becomes even in the midst of multiple voices.

Currently, 6 years after the project was given room in our hearts, the Cherish project now consists of 30 acres of land on the shores of Lake Victoria, a staff of 60 nationals, and 43 healthy, happy children, many of whom were hours away from death when they arrived on our doorstep. Beyond that is a school that educates 132 children from the poorest families in the surrounding district, and many other amazing projects.

We balance on a wire of faith every day as we continue to develop the project, but that's what faith is sometimes...

...a tightrope walk.

Sometimes, the way that you know that something is from God is that if you're wrong, it will fail.

We and the team that God used to build Cherish were able to build this project in faith because we'd been practicing faith throughout our lives on our own needs, our own family, our own environment.

You can't speak life into the great things until speaking life into every day things comes as naturally to you as speaking your primary language. We are so afraid of sounding stupid or making a mistake or being (heaven forbid) wr-wr-wr-wrong, that we often won't allow ourselves to even attempt speaking life over dead circumstances just in case nothing happens. Often the failure to speak life is more about our fear and pride, our horror of being disappointed again, than it is about the situation. Often our failure to break through in faith is directly attributable to our reluctance to speak in faith. What will happen if we fail?

Why are we so afraid of failure, as though it was a disease that intelligent/spiritual people don't catch? We all fail, and failure teaches us so much more than success does. For a start, it hones our ability to understand where we went wrong. Many great and godly people are so afraid of making a mistake that they never get around to making anything much.

Rick and I have a saying: **A job worth doing is worth doing badly at first.**

This doesn't mean that shoddy workmanship is okay. On the contrary, it means that nothing worth building is built perfectly from the start, but you do have to make a beginning and do the best you can and not be afraid of other people's judgements and criticisms while you're building. Many self-criticisms we make are only because we want to say those things first before anyone else can say them about us! So many great projects are aborted or never begun because of our own negative words, spoken over ourselves and our projects before someone else, whether parent, partner, friend or colleague, can say them.

When Nehemiah was building the wall around Jerusalem to protect it from the enemy onslaught, his team consisted of jewellers, perfumers and other non-skilled labourers. That wall must have looked less than perfect in places. But when Sanballat and Tobiah came to jeer, telling him the wall was so badly built that if even a fox ran over it, it would fall down, Nehemiah didn't stop to pay them attention. When they called to him to come to a meeting with them, so they could point out how woefully inadequate he/ his work was, he refused, telling them that he wouldn't stop the "great work" he was doing in order to come and listen to their negative, toxic opinions. Nehemiah never claimed that he was great at doing the work. No, it was the work he was doing, the work that God had commissioned him for, that was a great work. In doing the best he could, Nehemiah was relying on the fact that God would undertake to make up the difference so that the finished result was indeed great (Nehemiah 4; 6:1-3).

It's important when you're learning to speak the language of life to realise that you will get it wrong sometimes and your pride will suffer, but that's okay. Our pride needs every blow it gets. Stamp on its head. Kick it until it dies. Nothing terrible is going to happen if you get it wrong while you're practicing. God isn't into the bolt of lightning thing. He's not Thor! He's a great parent who loves it when His kids are trying to learn to speak His language and He helps them when they stumble over their words at times.

A church or an individual can learn to believe God for great things by practicing in small and personal things. You can't do something great for God until your faith in Him has accomplished great things in your own life, no matter how small they appear to other people. Destiny isn't set in stone. It's subject to our emotions, and fear, pride and apathy work together to destroy destiny. It's easy to subvert the purposes of God for your life just through allowing fear, the desire for comfort or security, or the need for approval to dissuade you from doing what God has said to do. More of the purposes of God have been aborted by people refusing to go ahead than any other reason.

God has called you to do some amazing things. Not everyone else may see and realise how amazing those things are, but He sees it all and it's important that we realise that we are playing out our life to an audience of One. Sometimes we give up too quickly because it costs so much in terms of our time, emotion, money … and we feel like we don't have the energy to carry it through. But God is calling you and He will enable you to fly, if you let Him. Whatever you go through is worth it to establish the Kingdom of God in your own life.

Nothing is ever wasted! God is the ultimate Recycler. No brokenness, no failures, no loss has the power to stop you from going forward, if you can learn to speak life into your own dry bones.

Flying is easy … once you get the hang of it.

5
How Not To
Speak Death

Avoiding the Henny Penny Syndrome

*"You cannot run away from weakness; you must some time fight it
out or perish; and if that be so, why not now...
and where you stand?"*
~Robert Louis Stevenson

*"Some people say they haven't yet found themselves. But the self
is not something one finds; it is something one creates."*
~Thomas Szasz

Life is made up of choices. We understand that our own lives are
governed by the choices we make, but often we don't appreciate
just how much our choices extend to influence the people around
us. It's a bit like viral advertising. If your perspective on a situation
or an event is significant enough to convince people in your circle
of influence, then they are likely to act on it and will probably

influence their other friends. When this happens, pretty soon, you have a culture shift.

The panic that ensued over the outbreak of swine flu is a good example. Intense media pressure played on people's fears to the point where every little cough and sniffle made people worry about the onset of the disease and possible imminent death.

Fashion brands have a similar effect. Adults as well as teenagers are convinced that without the right sneakers or handbag they are doomed to a life of ignominy. For many of us, it's the brands we carry that make up our story and our story shapes our world far more than we can know.

The children's story Henny Penny encapsulates this kind of herd-mentality thinking. Henny Penny was the hen who panicked when she was hit on the head by a pebble while scratching around in the barnyard. Convinced the sky was falling, she knew she had to go straight to the King and tell him. If she'd done that immediately she would have been fine, but on the way she met Chicken Licken.

Stopping to talk, she explained how the sky had become unstable and a piece of it had already fallen off and hit her on the head. Chicken Licken, who was of a nervous disposition himself and a bit of a drama queen, opted to go with her.

As they went on their journey, they met a large number of farmyard birds, including Cocky Locky, Ducky Lucky, Goosey Loosey, Gander Pander and Turkey Lurkey, all of whom they shared their panic with. What began as Henny Penny's personal phobia became widespread panic in the barnyard as the gaggle of feathered friends stumbled toward the King's palace until, stressed and exhausted, they finally had to stop and rest.

Fear has incredible power to drain the strength out of even the most fervent believer.

As they sat gabbling about what would happen when the ultimate nightmare came to pass and the whole sky fell to the earth, who should come along but that most cunning of villains, Foxy Loxy, who was naturally curious to find such a large dinner apparently waiting for him. He asked how they knew the sky was falling and they all began answering together, telling how they had each been told by someone, who'd been told by someone else. As it became clearer that the story had begun with Henny Penny, she eagerly took centre stage, cackling in a curious mixture of terror and pride about how a piece of the sky had fallen on her head.

Foxy Loxy knew a good deal when he saw it. Softly humming "I feel like Chicken Tonight" under his breath, he offered to show them a shortcut to the King's palace. The feeble-hearted farm fowls failed to remember that Jesus Christ is the only way to the King and they followed him to his den among the rocks. Just as the little group began crowding into the dark, narrow opening, following Foxy Loxy to their death, a little squirrel leapt out from behind a rock and yelled a warning to them. Suddenly they realised what was about to happen and they turned to run.

Seeing dinner disappearing, Foxy Loxy managed to grab hold of Henny Penny's tail feathers, but the squirrel threw a rock and hit him fair and square on the head. Screaming in pain and shock, Foxy Loxy dropped the chicken and ran into the cave shouting, "It's true! The sky is falling." The terrified birds wasted no time and ran as fast as they could to the King's palace where, gasping and panting, they managed to blurt out their dreadful news. The King waited until they quietened down before asking why they thought the sky was falling.

Now came Henny Penny's finest hour. She'd lived in insignificance all her life, but finally, her numerous fears were about to be validated and she knew that hereafter and forever (however short forever might be, seeing as they were threatened with imminent destruction) she would always be spoken of as the wise and understanding hen who really knew the score.

* * *

It's amazing how many people derive their identity from being a drama queen or a doomsayer. Combining a curious mixture of fear and self-importance, their negative predictions give them the recognition they crave, despite the fact that they so often undermine the purposes of God in their own lives and the lives of others. So often they derail the great things that God has purposed, but they never take responsibility for it, merely seeing their role as pointing out what could go wrong and then stepping back and detaching themselves from the confusion and fear they have caused.

* * *

Stepping up to the throne, Henny Penny showed the King the bump on her head and gabbled out her story of how a piece of the falling sky had landed right on top of her. The King leaned over and gently plucked out the small pebble that still rested among her feathers.

The sky wasn't falling at all. The world wasn't about to end. Henny Penny's bump would eventually go away and the world and the sky were still under the King's control.

The King has an amazing way of giving the right perspective. We get overwhelmed with the negativity of life and circumstances and we panic. We know we should go directly to the King, but on the way we stop to share our fear and depression with anyone who will listen – and many of them believe our report, because it's a lot easier to believe bad news than it is to see things from God's perspective and speak life – unless you've been practicing to live a life of faith. Suddenly we find ourselves surrounded by overwhelmed people who have been rendered powerless by rumours and half-truths. We forget that God promises that He is with us no matter what happens.

Those barnyard birds almost died because of their fear, their wrong perspective and their inclination to believe the negative without consulting the King, even though what they understood was wrong.

We need people who have God's perspective in the middle of turmoil and pressure. Unfortunately, we live in a society where many of us base our identity on the fact that "my situation is worse than yours … my story is more painful … my feelings have suffered more … whatever has happened to you has happened to me too – but it caused ten times more damage…" We compete to establish who is worse off!

Speaking life isn't automatic. Like other languages, it's learned. But it must be learned first in the heart, because it's the heart that directs our actions. When the heart has God's perspective, it can translate the language of life into our thinking. If we only learn it in our minds, it is merely positive speaking and there's no more life in positive speaking than there is in negative speaking.

If you're not speaking life, you won't bring life. Life is a language of the heart.

"The heart of the wise teaches the mouth [to speak]*…"* (Proverbs 16:23)

The first lesson to learn in speaking life, therefore, is how not to speak death.

Henny Penny and her friends were so far from speaking life that their language was death and their words were almost the death of them. It's so easy to automatically go to the most negative scenario possible, without having any concept that the fight of faith requires that we go to God and then couch our language accordingly, from His perspective, combined with our willingness to believe Him rather than the evidence of our senses.

Often the first lessons we need to learn in speaking life are...

...what *not* to say ...and *when* not to say it.

"And Moses said to the people, 'Fear not, stand firm, and see the salvation of the Lord, which He will work for you today. For the Egyptians whom you see today, you shall never see again. The Lord will fight for you, and you have only to be silent.'" (Exodus 14:13-14)

The Israelites were feeling great! Freedom was their current reality and they knew they would never go back to Egypt again. Then they realised the entire Egyptian army was behind them and that they were trapped between the devil and the deep blue sea.

"Then the Lord said to Moses, 'Tell the people of Israel to turn back and encamp in front of Pihahiroth, between Migdol and the sea ... for Pharaoh will say of the people of Israel, "they are wandering in the land; the wilderness has shut them in."'" (Exodus 14:1-3)

They'd been having such a great time celebrating that they hadn't realised that the fight to be free wasn't over yet. It's easy to get lulled into a false sense of security when we've fought a hard battle and won it. We think there comes a time when we're free and clear forever, but ... being trapped is always on the inside of us, not the outside.

If you can be free of fear, guilt, rage, lust, self-pity, negativity, intimidation, selfishness, pride and resentment on the inside, you'll be free no matter what your outer circumstances are. There are times when it feels to us like Pharaoh's opinion of the Israelites' situation mirrors ours. It really seems like "the wilderness has shut us in". Our enemy shouts that into our heart, but he's too late, we already think it ourselves.

It's vital to remember that the wilderness has no power to shut us in ... unless we let it. Jesus wasn't shut in by His time in the wilderness. On the contrary, it was there He established that what He'd been learning over the years was genuine and could be relied upon – that the word of God could be used as both a defensive and offensive weapon against His enemy.

We all regularly experience times when we have an opportunity to prove that what we've said we believe is really what we do believe. Despite what we say, it's what we do that is the final arbiter of what we actually believe. When we're not being challenged it's easy to spout scripture and make bold statements of faith. If we can do the same when there is a giant parading before us, daring us to fight, that's when we know that what we believe is solid and strong in our hearts.

Think about it.

The wilderness isn't a trap, it's like exam time. It establishes whether what we've learned about God's word and about ourselves is really true or whether it's just head knowledge. It's easy to quote Scriptures and principles without having lived them. But when the pressure is on, it becomes obvious that we don't really believe what we've said.

What we do is what we believe, not what we say.

* * *

God was about to do some amazing stuff with Israel and part of His strategy was for everyone to ... shut up!

"The Lord will fight for you, and you have only to be silent." (Exodus 14:14)

Some translations say, "hold your peace", which is literally what ceasing to speak would help them to do. If peace is a Christian characteristic, it's important to realise there is a strong connection between trusting God enough to not speak out how things look, and staying in the place of peace.

To have the peace that passes all understanding...

...you have to give up your right to understand!

Imagine it! Several million men, women and children are camped in front of the Red Sea with the enemy about half a mile behind them, and no place to go...

...and Moses says, "Don't worry. Stand firm and watch God save you. The enemy who has enslaved and brutalised you and your families for generations is about to disappear because God is fighting for you. All you have to do is SHUT UP!"

It was the same strategy God used when the walls came down at Jericho.

In Joshua 6:10 Joshua tells the people they are not to speak until he says they can – and they held their peace for seven days! Could you do that when you have a really clear opinion about the situation you're in?

What would your opinion be? Would it add faith to the process of those walls coming down or the sea opening up, or would it state the bloomin' obvious as far as normal life was concerned? Would your opinion take into account that God is at work in the situation?

The story of the Israelites coming out of captivity is a fantastic example for the Church. Paul talks about the problem they had with their words.

"We must not put Christ to the test, as some of them did and were destroyed by serpents, nor grumble, as some of them did and were destroyed by the Destroyer." (1 Corinthians 10:9-10)

How we speak about what we're going through has incredible power to decide our future. Paul says that complaining and grumbling gives room for the Destroyer to destroy. Choosing not to speak death isn't denial. Henny Penny could have said, "Wow, what just hit me on the head? That really hurt!" But instead she immediately jumped to the worst possible scenario and convinced herself and everyone around her that the world was about to end.

She and the friends she influenced were almost killed through the power of her words. The fact that she was wrong was irrelevant. It was her wrong perspective that herded them into the position that could have easily have made them into packets of Foxy's Fowl Feed.

You might have more bills than money right now, but learning to speak life means that your words will express your trust in God to provide your needs. Reminding yourself that He has done it before and that His word promises that you will not lack any good thing will give you the strength to believe. You might have health issues, but your choice to call on Jehovah Rapha, the God who heals, rather than doom yourself to infirmity or death through words of fear and anguish, will strengthen your capacity to believe God for your healing.

We have such a tendency to "awfulise"! We use our words to make our situation awfuller than it really is. Literally, we exercise our faith to see the situation get worse.

The media does it every day. Remember Y2K? The newspapers and TV reports were so positive that all the computers across the world were going to shut down, because they wouldn't have the capacity to turn over from 1999 to 2000. Now it seems laughable, but at the time fear was being peddled all around the world. People, including Christians, stored up food and provisions and even weapons, ready for a worldwide shutdown ...

...that never happened.

(A few simple-minded people such as myself wondered why no one had invented a computer that knew how to turn over the page from one millennium to the next. As it turned out, they had.)

The media trumpets bird flu, swine flu, floods, tsunamis, the credit crunch and every other ugly thing that happens across the planet. Rarely, if ever, do they tell us about anything good. Why? Because bad news sells so much better than good news. Why? Because there's something intrinsically wrong with our hearts that has a magnetic attraction to what is wrong rather than what is right. That's why we gossip, criticise, complain, exaggerate and focus on how bad things are – with ourselves and with everyone else, too.

"Finally brothers, whatever is true, whatever is honourable, whatever is just, whatever is pure, whatever is lovely, whatever is commendable, if there is any excellence, if there is any thing worthy of praise, think about these things." (Philippians 4:8)

Remember, speaking life is not about being in denial. But we all know how easy it is to get bogged down in conversations, speaking about things we wanted that we didn't get, instead of reciting how we've been blessed and encouraged and what has been given to us that we didn't deserve. It's about thankfulness versus a grumbling heart.

Proverbs 18:21 says,

"Death and life are in the power of the tongue and those who love it will eat its fruits." (Proverbs 18:21)

Literally, that means you get to ingest and then digest what you've created by your repetitive conversation, because what you keep on saying becomes part of your world.

It becomes your identity.

Making yourself the victim of circumstances may get you sympathy and some extra attention for a time, but if that's the way you live your life you'll end up as a helpless victim of circumstance rather than someone whose strength is in the Lord. Not only that, but you'll be a total bore as well!

We don't have to live in denial. We live in a real world where bad stuff happens to good people. People do lose their jobs, their homes, their health, their relationships and it would be stupid to deny that...

...but it doesn't have to end there.

The principle of speaking life is actually an expression of trusting God in the midst of everything. Speaking life isn't being deluded, it's choosing to trust the God who spoke light into your life because He loves you. He promises to care and provide for you.

Christians are called to change our cultures. How we behave in difficult times dictates whether we will change the culture...

...or whether it will change us.

Christians all over the world are living out this message of trust in God despite persecution and even death. Our circumstances aren't the issue. It's about whether we can see our circumstances from God's perspective.

6
The Devil Knows Your Language

How to listen to God when you're under siege

"Build me a son, O Lord, who will be strong enough to know when he is weak, and brave enough to face himself when he is afraid. One who will be proud and unbending in honest defeat, and humble and gentle in victory."
~Douglas MacArthur

"Be your own palace, or the world is your jail."
~John Donne

One of Judah's best kings was Hezekiah. For most of his life, everything he did was right. He honoured God and showed it by cleaning out the Temple and repairing its great doors, shut for so long under the reign of his apostate father, Ahaz. His actions turned the hearts of the people back to their Lord as he made incredible sacrifices and tore down the shrines of the false idols worshiped by previous kings. He had the wellbeing of his people at heart, leading them back into the practice of keeping the Passover. He established worship as an integral part of the priests' lifestyle, and his godly leadership brought the nation back to a renewal of their worship of God.

His father had led the nation into subjection to Assyria, the superpower of the day, but Hezekiah rebelled against the king of Assyria, refusing to allow his people to be enslaved any more. His war with the Philistines paralleled David's military prowess. He was an amazing man who trusted God to the point that the teller of his story exults: *"There was none like him among the kings of Judah, either before or after him."* (2 Kings 18:5)

Sometimes, when you hear people talk about the role that faith in Christ plays in our lives, you could get the impression that if you love God and do the right thing, no bad or difficult things will ever happen to you. I think we've all found out by now that nothing could be further from the truth. Tough, ugly, devastating and frightening things happen to good people. We all come under siege at times and when that happens, it challenges us to know whether what we said we believe is what we really do believe.

Hezekiah had been ruling well and then the enemy rocked up on his doorstep to reclaim the rebellious nation of Judah. That Assyrian king was going to teach Hezekiah a lesson for daring to defy him.

Hezekiah had won many battles earlier in his reign, in the days when he had no other option beyond trusting in God. But by the time the Assyrian army arrived he was older and had become much more comfortable with his role as king. He'd got into the rhythm of ruling and had lost the edge he once had when his passion and lack of experience motivated him to follow God without question.

Comfort generally has more power to keep us out of the fight than fear does.

Hezekiah was no longer prepared to fight, which is strange considering he was the one who'd started the battle in the first place by breaking away from Assyria's rule. Despite his brave decision, he now concluded that discretion was a better option than valour, so he looked for ways to compromise. He wanted to avoid the inevitable fight.

By the way … avoidance of a fight by compromising doesn't exist anywhere except in our imaginations. Some time, somewhere, we must make a stand or lose everything.

In his earlier years, when the worship of God had been his priority, Hezekiah had spent a lot of effort and money keeping the Temple decorated as befitted the House of God. He'd overlaid the internal doors and doorposts with gold, and the treasuries were full of silver and precious stones. His compromise allowed the king of Assyria to name his price, however, and it was huge. He demanded three hundred talents of silver and thirty talents of gold.

That's a lot of bullion! Where was he going to get that kind of money? From the Temple, of course! Hezekiah raided the treasury, taking out the precious things he'd once laboured to furnish the place, including stripping the gold that he'd lined the doors with.

As a young woman I was hot-tempered and difficult, always carrying grudges and making life difficult for everyone around me. In the years since I became a Christian, God has helped me to change, turning me into a forgiver, someone who values grace and mercy and someone who values relationship.

I've become someone who knows the language of life. He really did that. Ask the people who knew me then and still know me now.

It wasn't easy. There were many intense battles in which I wrestled with God over my tendency to judge myself by my intentions and everyone else by their actions. While I focused on everyone else's problems, He focused on my lack of mercy and grace, and the plank in my own eye. Gradually, the longer I have known Him and the more influence He has had on my life, I have changed. Practice really does make perfect and I not only learned to say sorry when I needed to, and forgive when I needed to, I also learned to prefer forgiveness to the alternative.

Human beings were never designed to carry the weight of unforgiveness. It makes us sick, stressed and unhappy when we try to, no matter how justified we feel.

"Or do you not know that your body is a temple of the Holy spirit within you, whom you have from God? You are not your own." (1 Corinthians 6:19)

Since Jesus was resurrected, His home is no longer a special building where we all go to visit Him. We are now His Temple. He lives in us by His Holy Spirit and we, like the good priests and kings of the Old Testament, are decorating the inside of our temples with the precious revelations He is giving us as He changes us to make us more like Him.

Every time I chose to forgive someone instead of bearing a grudge, that godly choice put another layer of gold on the inside of my Temple. Every time I pushed through to give what I wanted to keep for myself, another layer of gold was added. When I sacrificed my own desires in order to obey God, more precious metal was inlaid in my Temple. The old me kept changing; I became a new creation (2 Corinthians 5:17).

As time went on and more personal battles were won, the layers of gold increased. In every area God was transforming me from glory to glory by His Spirit (2 Corinthians 3:18). The gold in my Temple was hard won through many spiritual battles – and it was all the more precious because of the struggles I had to go through to win it. I stopped categorising people in a way that gave me the room or right to dislike them. I genuinely accepted the people around me, even when I didn't agree with them and even when I didn't classify them as particular friends. I loved people because I had learned to walk in the forgiveness of myself, which meant I could forgive other people. Even though they were not my friends, per se, they were people I genuinely appreciated and valued.

The degree to which you accept and value yourself is in direct proportion to the degree to which you will accept and value other people. As God changed my heart, I began to value who I was in Him, no longer wishing I was like someone else and no longer trying to be what I was not. I was glad to be me. I liked myself.

Jesus told us to love our neighbour as we love ourselves. Many of us find that a difficult scripture and yet, the truth is, if we don't love ourselves, God help our neighbour. The people who are able to accept others most freely are those who have come to terms with themselves in Christ, accepting and appreciating the way God has made them.

We gain those layers of gold in so many ways. Every time we give instead of hoard, every time we choose the truth instead of lying, every time we lay our lives down to obey God and serve His ways instead of our own, another layer of gold is inlaid across the inner sanctum of our personal Temple. It's so exhilarating to realise how much you've grown and changed because of the purposes of God at work in your heart and in your life. When you're transformed like that, it can seem that nothing will ever be able to take away those victories and the preciousness of what has happened to change you and make you more like Jesus.

But the Temple needs upkeep. The gold doesn't just stay there of its own accord. It has to be guarded vigilantly. There's always an enemy on your doorstep demanding compromise, looking for ways to steal away the goldenness of the graces that have been painstakingly inlaid in your life.

There's always another battle to challenge whether you still really believe what you say you believe.

There came a time when I was tired of fighting; tired of the battle; tired of having to get my heart right all the time; tired of having to be the mature one. It was a strategic moment for compromise.

We were pastoring our first church and we had a lady (as happens in every church) who was very difficult to get on with. She often had me backed into a corner, always sounding off about something she was irritated by. I genuinely managed to be gracious and answer her with a loving spirit – mainly because I truly tried to understand her, where she was coming from, and I could forgive her because I knew that she had her own issues.

This day was different though. I was tired, irritated and sick of bearing the brunt of other people's issues. As I stood listening to another tirade of anger and judgement pouring out of her mouth, a thought came unbidden into my mind … and I let it stay.

The thought was this: *I don't like you.* Even as I thought it, I felt relief. Nothing in my face or manner changed towards her, but I felt somehow gratified that I had allowed myself the luxury of disliking her. After all, she was only one person and God knew I was justified in feeling that way.

A few months later, I found myself trapped in a conversation at a pastors' conference with a leader who was sounding forth on his favourite subject – himself. As I sat and listened to his legalistic, self-centred conversation, another thought came to me. Even though months had passed between this thought and the previous one, it felt like it followed on just a few seconds later.

The thought was this: *...And I don't like you either.* Again, I felt okay about my decision. Six months later, I was crying on my husband's shoulder telling him how unhappy I was with who I was becoming. I didn't like myself any more and I was tired, disillusioned and frustrated with so many of the relationships around me. I wept, saying: *I've got so many issues with so many people. It feels as though I don't like anyone any more.*

Light broke through my darkness as I said it. I remembered the two times I had given myself permission to dislike someone that God loves. All those battles I'd fought over the years to become more like Christ, loving and accepting the people He loves and accepts, had been rendered null and void just because I had allowed myself the luxury of choosing who I had the right to reject.

I'd spent years fighting battles in my heart to be changed. Each skirmish won had placed another layer of gold on the doors of my heart, the place where God dwelt. And then in a season of tiredness, frustration and hurt, I compromised what I knew to be right and had begun the process of stripping the revelation of His love and grace away from my inner self to give it to the enemy who had set up a siege at my door.

The trouble is, compromise always looks more like the answer than it actually turns out to be.

In Hezekiah's case (and in mine), instead of going away when he was paid off, the enemy moved in and captured the fortified cities, and now they were coming up against Jerusalem. The king saw his compromise hadn't worked and realised, almost too late, that he had to make a stand now before he lost everything he'd worked so hard to win over the time of his reign.

He sent out his head guys to hear the message spoken by the chief official of the Assyrian army ... which was to advise them to give up.

"And the Rabshakeh said to them, 'Say to Hezekiah, "thus says the great king, the King of Assyria: On what do you rest this trust of yours? Do you think that mere words are strategy and power for war? In whom do you now trust, that you have rebelled against me?"'" (Isaiah 36:4-5)

He went on to taunt them about their inability to fight, saying it was their own God who sent him to conquer them. Hezekiah's team were stressed because he was speaking in the language of the people and they could understand the threats. They pleaded with him to speak in Aramaic, a language known only to them and not the common people. Obviously, their request was refused and the Rabshakeh redoubled his efforts to persuade them to give up, telling the people not to listen to Hezekiah who was encouraging them to trust in the Lord. No other god of any other conquered nation had been able to save its people from Assyria, so how could tiny Judah stand a chance?

His tone changed, becoming much more friendly as he promised that if they made peace with him, nothing much would change. They could sit under that same tree they'd always sat under; they could eat the same fruit and drink the same wine. Even when he took them away to captivity, the land they would go to was not all that different from their own land. Everything would still be the same.

Except they would be slaves!

No one answered. The king had commanded them not to speak. There's a key in this story that is easy to miss, and it's this:

The devil knows your language and he is able to speak it fluently to you.

The head guys wanted the enemy to speak in a language the people didn't know, but he's never going to do that. He wants us to understand. He wants to terrify and overwhelm us. He wants to disappoint us and drive us to despair. That's why he goes to the trouble of learning our language.

The language he learns isn't our native language. It's not English or German or Swahili or Indonesian. It's the language of our hearts and minds. The devil deliberately learns the language that our hearts will listen to and respond to.

He knows what you worry about. He knows the things that will cause you to stress out when you think about them. He knows how anxiety builds up the longer you dwell on something. He knows the temptations that come and dance around in your mind when you least expect them and he knows how desperate you feel when that happens. He doesn't play fair. He has no mercy for you or anyone else. He has no good side that can be appealed to when you feel like you need a break from the pressure. His mission is to destroy your life and your destiny.

He has a plan for you and it's a distortion of what God wants for you. It's a plan for evil and not for good, to take away your hope and your future (his version of Jeremiah 29:11). He looks at your situation, evaluates what might work and is endlessly patient and willing to keep trying different strategies until he finds the tactics that succeed, and then he follows through on those.

Our minds are the breeding ground for the fruit of our lives. What we allow ourselves to think is who we become.

The world is full of all sorts of stuff that we don't want to take on board or even think about, but the devil makes sure that we get the opportunity to think about those things whether we want to or not. Have you ever wondered where that random, unbidden, unclean thought came from? Have you ever wondered why you suddenly felt jealous over someone else's blessing, when in reality, you wouldn't even want it if you were given it? Have you been shocked at how quickly fear can strike your heart?

We have an enemy that stands outside our minds with flaming thought bombs that he fires at us with random efficiency. In his arsenal are all the thoughts we don't want: shame, fear, lust, anger, depression, selfishness, hatred, apathy, pride, laziness, bitterness, comparison, spite, discouragement, greed, self pity, and whatever else you can think of.

When a person is dealing rightly with their thought life, they'll throw the thought back out again with energy, taking every thought captive to the knowledge of Jesus Christ (2 Corinthians 10:5).

That thought comes bouncing back at the devil's feet and when it happens regularly with specific thoughts, he knows that that particular type of issue is not going to work for him to bring you down. He may bombard you with shame, pride, selfishness, fear and apathy and you deal immediately with shame, selfishness, and apathy, but pride and fear stay in there.

He knows your weak spots by what you didn't throw back out! So those are the things he keeps working on in order to bring you down.

Fear and pride go hand in hand. Letting those thoughts remain looks like this:

"If people knew this about me, they wouldn't accept me. I can't let them see what I'm really like."

Rejection teams well with pride:

"Why didn't they choose me? I'm much better than her. They are obviously against me."

When fear and pride and rejection work together, it's easy for bitterness to join in.

"They'll never choose me anyway. They don't like me. I don't belong with them. They don't think I'm good enough. I need to go where I'm appreciated. I may as well live how I want to live. No one cares about me anyway. I deserve a bit of comfort."

And lust joins the crowd, whispering, *"Just once won't hurt. You've got it under control. No one will know. You deserve some comfort for all the pain you've gone through."*

And so it goes. We've fought hard to grow and change and become more like Jesus, lining our inner Temple with the gold of a character that is looking more and more like Him. And then, in a weak moment when we're sick of fighting, compromise suddenly presents itself as our best option. If we believe it, the process of stripping our hard won gold away from our Temple begins. Without realising it, all the precious revelation begins to erode as we systematically strip away first one and then another layer of the gold that has made so much difference in the way we conduct our life.

We all have the same issues. They push and crowd into our thoughts, jostling against each other for position in the front row of our thinking. The enemy easily works out what thoughts are more likely to stay in our minds, what language we speak in our hearts, simply by taking notice of what we reject. He speaks our language, just like the Assyrian spoke the language of Judah, knowing that his words struck fear in their hearts.

He wanted them to surrender without a fight.

He wants you to surrender without a fight.

The people understood when he told them the gods of their neighbours hadn't been able to help them, and he cleverly played on their fears about whether their God could or would make the difference for them. They were all aware of their neighbours. They could identify with what those people hoped for and put their trust in, what their ambitions and fears were. Despite their love for God, they were heavily influenced by the atmosphere of the society around them that was driven by fear, anxiety, pressure, greed, lust, pride, shame, bitterness, family expectations. These things are common to us all. The enemy doesn't just bombard people's minds with his godless thoughts – he attacks society with them as well, and we are all influenced by the society we are part of, no matter how spiritual we think we are. We have no idea how entrenched in certain thinking patterns we are, just because that's the default position of our society.

Not only that, but in every generation some of the heroes of Church life, great men and women of faith, have fallen morally, tumbling headlong off the pedestals we've put them on, and that scares us too. We looked up to them; we drew strength and revelation from what they said. If they couldn't keep fighting the good fight when they were so strong and spiritual, how can we expect to? We are afraid because we see the reflection of our own weaknesses in the weaknesses of others and wonder how anyone can succeed when our heroes didn't.

Christians are no different to anyone else, except in one way.

We have more to draw from than our own internal resources. We have a relationship with the One who can help us defeat the pressures everyone suffers from. It's easy to quote the Bible when times are okay, but does it actually work when you're up against it?

Well, you tell me!

Every Christian has to work that out for himself. All the preachers in the world can give you the Five Point Plan for Avoiding Sin, but when the enemy is speaking to you in your language, no matter what the subject is and no matter how mature and wise you've been up to now, you will see by your choices whether what you say you believe is actually what you do believe.

No matter how mature or well known we are, when the enemy is speaking our language there is only one course of action to save us from the fear, depression or lust that is threatening to swallow us whole. Like Hezekiah and his subjects, it's then that we must go to God rather than enter into a conversation with the enemy.

"As soon as Hezekiah heard it, he tore his clothes and covered himself with sackcloth and went into the house of the Lord." (Isaiah 37:1)

Hezekiah did what he should have done in the first place ... and what he used to do in the good old days when he wasn't tired of being focused on the purposes of God. He went straight to the Temple himself and he sent his leaders to the prophet to hear what God was saying. The stripping back of the gold he had laid in the Temple had caused more problems instead of solving them. He was looking to the Lord again.

Isaiah tells us that God had a strategy to cause the invading army to turn back, but not before they wrote an intimidating letter to Hezekiah telling him they would be back. Hezekiah read the letter, acknowledging the situation (remember, denial isn't faith) and then showed it to God, spreading it out in the Temple.

What might happen if we did the same? What if we took the things that threaten and intimidate us and physically spread them out in front of God? Try it with your bills.

In the midst of the terror, God answered Hezekiah. He sent an angel into the enemy camp and 185,000 men were killed overnight. Sennacherib went home and was killed by his own sons as he worshiped in the temple of the god he said would defeat Judah's God. It's true that the devil knows our language, but it's even truer that God is able to overrule whatever he says to us, if we will trust Him instead of what we are hearing. The devil's language is negative and damaging, hateful and selfish, but the Word of God is a sharp, double-edged sword, able to destroy the work of the enemy.

"For the law of the spirit of Life in Christ Jesus has made you free from the law of sin and death." (Romans 8:2)

How does that work?

Think of the law of gravity versus the law of aerodynamics. Gravity is an incontrovertible fact. Nothing will stop the Mac I'm typing on from falling off the desk and landing on the floor if I accidentally knock it off, and that's the way it has been for all time.

Until something amazing happened. Someone discovered the law of aerodynamics, which overruled and superseded the law of gravity. Which means that even though flying is impossible ...

...You can fly if you want to.

Our lives mirror Hezekiah's. The enemy comes against us to tell us all the things that are wrong. He itemises long lists for us detailing how we've failed and where we've failed and why we won't make it and where we've lost out ... and a lot of it may be true.

And our King says to us the same thing Hezekiah said to his people: "Don't answer him. Don't get caught up in conversation with him [like Eve did] ... Come here to me." Take what the enemy has said to you and spread it out in front of your God. He's got a strategy and He promises that if you will listen to Him and not the enemy, you will win that battle. Part of God's strategy is the way we speak. Remember what the Rabshakeh said?

*"Do you think that **mere words** are strategy and power for war?"* (Isaiah 36:5)

Well, God thinks words are a great strategy and contain much power to war against the enemy. He says His Word is a sword (Ephesians 6:17) and when we choose to use the sword against the work of the enemy, we will see breakthrough and victory.

The Word of God is our strategy and power for war.

It's a fact of life that we've all failed and continue to do so. There are areas of shame and brokenness in our lives that threaten to overwhelm us. The devil tries to entice us into compromise and he mocks us and screams at us in the way we will most easily understand, telling us we may as well just give up; that surrender won't be as bad as we've been told. Just lay down your weapons and your problems will be over and the new place you will live in will be just as good as the place you fought to win in Christ.

He doesn't tell you that you'll be a slave there.

He knows how to discourage and defeat us, telling us there's no point in struggling. He knows the words to use to seduce us into thinking *just one more won't hurt* and *it's not really destroying my life, my relationships and my future.* He's subtle. He would much rather talk than fight, especially if your fight entails using the word of God.

The power he has isn't in the difficult things that happen to you. Hard and painful things happen to everyone. His power is in whether he can persuade you to deal with your life his way. Don't listen to him. He learned your language with the specific intention of destroying you. Do what Hezekiah did and take it to God.

It's true that you can be accused of many things, but that's why Jesus died for you. Being under siege is not the issue. We all experience seasons like that at different times and in different settings.

What makes the difference is who you surrender to in the midst of the fight.

7
An Unconquerable Church

Getting prophetic revelation directly from God

"The one who is going to associate intimately with God must go beyond all that is visible and (lifting up his own mind, as to a mountaintop, to the invisible and incomprehensible) believe that the divine is there where the understanding does not reach."
~Gregory of Nyssa

"Don't think so much about who is for or against you, rather give all your care that God be with you in everything you do."
~Thomas Kempis

In the latter part of His three and a half years of ministry, Jesus made the decision to up the game. The season was changing and it was time for those who followed Him to make the choice as to whether they could put their lives on the line over the identity of the One they were following. He selected the region of Caesarea

Philippi as the perfect place in which to have a strategic discussion with His disciples.

The dark city of Caesarea Philippi sat at the base of a cliff where it was commonly believed that the gates of the underworld were situated at the mouth of a cave. The city was originally a centre for the worship of the god Baal, who had subsequently been replaced by the Greek god Pan. At this time in history the now dead Julius Caesar had become the local god of choice. There was a huge level of demonic activity operating around the place because, in order to encourage their god to return to them each year, the people engaged in all manner of perverse and grotesque sexual deeds to attract him. The niches in the rocks were filled with idols. Rampant prostitution, paedophilia and bestiality were common in the city.

Regardless of the truth of the legend, the actions of the inhabitants of the city ensured that Caesarea Philippi truly was an open portal to hell.

Bizarrely and strategically Jesus had chosen to bring His disciples to the worst red light district imaginable in order to talk with them about His identity and His future plans for His Church! (Matthew 16:13-19)

As was His tendency, He began this prophetic conversation innocently enough by asking them what the crowds following them thought of Him. They'd obviously been talking together about it because several of them answered at once, telling Him that some people were saying He was John the Baptist resurrected, and others went even further back in history, saying He might be Elijah or Jeremiah. "So then," Jesus asked, fixing them with His clear and disconcerting gaze. "Who do you guys think I am?"

The silence was palpable, and then Peter blurted out what they'd all been discussing:

"You're the Christ! You're the Son of the Living God."

Jesus grinned, clapping Peter on the back in delight! High fives all round! "Blessed are you, Simon bar Jonah! For flesh and blood has not revealed this to you, but my Father who is in heaven. And I tell you, you are Peter, and on this rock, I will build my church, and the gates of hell shall not prevail against it." (Matthew 16:17-18)

This verse has puzzled Christians through the ages, with many people and denominations mistakenly believing that the rock mentioned was Peter himself. Yet it's clear that Peter was no better than any of us at getting life right and certainly didn't seem to have what it would take to be the platform on which the Church could be built. Without understanding the environment and the setting of the conversation, we are left with more questions than answers.

This whole section is a perfect example of the massive play on words God seems to enjoy using. Right there, at the supposed seat of the government of hell, Jesus deliberately led the conversation to the place where His followers would acknowledge to each other, to Him, and to every demonic entity, who He really was. When Jesus spoke about building His Church on such a foundation that the gates of hell would not prevail against it, He said it right on the very spot where those gates were reputed to stand! Symbolically, gates in the Bible refer to leadership, so as Jesus stood in the heart of enemy territory and described the attack that would be launched against evil by the Church, He was saying that there is nothing strong enough to prevail against a people who have a clear revelation of His true status as the Son of God.

Jesus' exhilaration at the answer Peter gave was not just because it was right, but because it established clearly that Peter was able to hear and receive revelation from Father God Himself. In other words, Peter's confession revealed a new understanding, a new platform or Rock, on which the Church of Jesus Christ would be established.

Jesus was saying that it is the spoken confession of people who receive revelation that He is the Son of God and Messiah which provides the strong foundation on which the Church will be built! The Church is not built on any person other than Himself, but Peter's confession showed that he had received revelation from God about Jesus' divinity and it is upon that understanding that the Church will be built and established.

This was what set the disciples of Jesus apart from the crowd that followed Him around. Instead of wondering, opinionating and gossiping about Him, Peter and the others who followed Jesus at close quarters had heard directly from God about the divinity of their Rabbi and had put their revelation into words that would stand for all time. This is the essence of the Church, a people who are set apart by the revelation they've received of the true and irrevocable Lordship of Jesus Christ.

This paved the way for another extraordinary event that was to take place in the lives of Jesus' followers. Jesus' power was rooted in His relationship with His Father. The healings, the supernatural wisdom, and the great power of His preaching all stemmed from His interaction with His Father who instructed and showed Him the truth of the issues beyond what was obvious to the five senses. Jesus was a man of great revelation. He heard God at every level and He acted on what He heard. There'd never been anyone like Him.

Previously, in the Old Testament times, the Holy Spirit came "on" someone for a specific task or season and left when the task was fulfilled. It was different with Jesus. He was filled with the Holy Spirit from the day He was baptised in water. From then on the triune God worked together in Him, giving Him freedom and spiritual understanding to move in revelation of God's will and way for whatever He was doing. As the first born of many brethren (Romans 8:29), the life of Jesus was opening up a new way for God-followers everywhere. The way Holy Spirit inhabited the life of Jesus set the stage for every disciple to have the same experience and Peter's confession ratified the new thing God was doing. On the day of Pentecost all the believers were filled with the Holy Spirit and He has come to live in waiting disciples ever since (Acts 2).

So Jesus was telling His disciples that their ability to obtain revelation from God about the Lordship of Christ was the rock of truth upon which He could build His Church. It was never about Peter. Even the most cursory reading of the New Testament makes it clear that although Peter was often a spokesman for the Church, he was just one of many leaders and certainly not superior to the others. Later New Testament books show that when a decision was to be made by the Jerusalem Council, although Peter had influence, it was Jesus' brother James who seemed to have the authority to give the final verdict (Acts 15:19). Peter struggled with jealousy over the closeness Jesus had with John (John 21:20-22).

There is nothing in any of the writings of the New Testament to suggest that Jesus was intending to risk the future destiny of the Church of the ages on the shoulders of one imperfect man, regardless of which of the disciples we might put forward as being more suited to leading the Church. Peter himself knew how easily he messed up and how often he misunderstood the issues at hand. At one point, Paul rebuked him publicly because Peter's fear of man caused him to act like a hypocrite when faced with racism between the Jews and the gentiles (Galatians 2:11-13).

In fact, just four verses on from the astonishing revelation of Jesus being the Messiah, Peter shows himself to be just as thick as ever. He had the temerity to start rebuking Jesus for speaking about the suffering and death that lay ahead of Him, something a disciple would ordinarily never do with his rabbi. His pride at being singled out as the guy with the huge revelation gave him some sort of idea that he could redirect the Lord's perspective of His future.

It hardly sounds like the guy that Jesus was betting all His chips on. He tells him very clearly that he is a hindrance because he'd stopped receiving revelation from God and had begun to think in worldly terms again.

It is Jesus who is called the foundation stone of the Church and, according to the apostle Paul (Ephesians 2:20), the ascension ministry gifts of apostles and prophets (of whom Peter is one among many) make up the rest of the foundation.

Just because we receive revelation and get it right at times, doesn't mean we remain right from that point on. If we don't keep pushing in to continue to hear from God, we quickly revert to our old ways of thinking. That's what happened to Peter.

Revelation isn't intellect, nor is it common sense, good judgement or education. People can receive huge revelation whether or not they are considered to be academically bright. A high intellect is not a prerequisite for a leader in the Body of Christ, but anyone who would lead God's people must have the capacity to hear from God and receive revelation from Him. It's a common failing of all disciples to hear from God on one point and then slip back into judging by our own opinions of what is right and wrong in other areas, totally missing what God is saying and doing. Martin Luther is a great example of this. This father of the faith who laid down his life to bring revelation to the Church on the matter of salvation by faith, was a hater of the Jews who tried to incite violence and death against them. We are all flawed. None of us have all the answers, which is why we have to hear from God to get His perspective on anything that relates to us. It's too easy to get carried away with our own opinions and miss out on what God thinks.

It happens all the time...

...to all of us.

Fluency in speaking life is rooted in prophetic conversations with God, and they are prophetic because they go beyond the shopping lists of prayer or the litany of woes we so commonly tend to recite. Life speakers hear from God in such a way as to gain His perspective for the way forward. They are prophetic because the conversation is built on relationship and not on pride, duty, need or prejudice. They are prophetic because they use what they hear to change the atmosphere they are surrounded by, rather than being engulfed by it.

Learning to speak life springs directly from hearing God speak it to you.

Standing right there, challenging the powers of darkness in what was deemed to be their own city, Jesus told Peter and the other disciples that He didn't make a move without hearing from His Father, and they shouldn't either. He could say that, now that He knew His disciples could hear from God for themselves, beginning with the revelation of His Lordship.

Our revelation of the Kingdom always begins with the revelation of the Lordship of Jesus Christ in our own lives.

"I will give you the keys of the kingdom of heaven; and whatever you bind (declare to be improper and unlawful) on earth, must be what is already bound in heaven; and whatever you loose (declare lawful) on earth must be what is already loosed in heaven." (Matthew 16:19)

Jesus affirmed to them that upon the rock of revelation they had received, He could build a Church that the gates of hell could not withstand. As a result, He could now give them the keys of the Kingdom, through which they would come to see the power of what it is to bind and loose on earth according to what has taken place in heaven.

The art of speaking life begins with prophetic conversations with God that then carry through to the natural realm, intersecting with people's lives and entering their circumstances and situations to bring God's perspective rather than our own or theirs. Jesus wanted His disciples to understand that following Him would be nothing less than an assault on hell, an assault which can never be fought on the inside of the Church. On the contrary, if the Church is to win the battle, and Jesus foretold that this will happen, it will be as each generation of the Church takes its place at the very gates of hell and advances from there.

Whoever holds the keys of any place is in charge; they have authority over whatever those keys lock and unlock. In this case, the keys are to the Kingdom of Heaven and just having the revelation of the Lordship of Christ in our hearts does away with any need for the keys to death and hell. Jesus already won them, which is why hell can't prevail against the Church.

8
How To Speak Life

...and not become like the place you are in

"Only your real friends will tell you when your face is dirty."
~Sicilian Proverb

"Everything can change, but not the language we carry inside us,
like a world more exclusive and final than one's mother's womb."
~Italo Calvino

As I mentioned earlier, when Rick and I first moved to Britain, God spoke to us from the scripture in Ezekiel 37 where Ezekiel's words performed a miracle, snatching life from the jaws of death. He made it clear to us that He has a plan for these islands and inherent in it was the need for us to do as Ezekiel did, speaking life into the heart of the nations and people of Great Britain.

As exhilarating as it was for us to think that God might use us to help bring change, the instruction came with a warning that if we didn't speak life into the dryness and death, dryness and death awaited us also.

Speaking the language of life isn't easy. There is a lot of work required to reverse the training we received from childhood. No matter what our native language, we all quickly pick up negative speak. From our earliest years we learn words of inadequacy, fear, anger, dishonesty, judgment, indecision, mocking, pride, false modesty, hinting, crudeness, lasciviousness, envy, cruelty, sarcasm, shame... Our manner of speaking develops according to our circumstances, our environment, our choices. Unbelievable as it may seem, our lifestyle adapts itself to our language.

Nothing about that will change unless we make the decision to change the way we speak.

Jesus speaks a different language to the world we live in – the language of life. Initially when we hear it, it sounds like a foreign language. In fact, many people are profoundly irritated by those who keep speaking positively despite their circumstances.

Jesus didn't speak scripture all the time. The words He spoke have become scripture, but His language wasn't scripture ... it was life. The scriptures contain life if we will speak them out over our circumstances. But the power isn't in the words that are said, it's in the LIFE that they carry.

Do your words carry life? If not, what DO they carry?

"Then He said to them, be careful what you hear. With the same measure you use, it will be measured to you." (Mark 4:24)

I've always been intrigued by this scripture, because at first glance it doesn't really make sense. How can we control what we hear? The words around us make their way unbidden into our senses. Whatever we are in earshot of, we can't help but hear. The point is, what we hear and how we hear has a tremendous impact on our thought life which, in turn, greatly influences what we go on to say … for other people to hear.

What do you hear?

Do people feel comfortable to criticise others when they're with you? Do they have liberty to take pot shots at their partner, your partner, your leaders, the boss, your friends, the church, the pastors, the kids, the task ahead, when they're in your company?

When you are in conversation, do you carefully dissect what is said in order to find and receive the full impact of anything negative? Are you waiting for some ripe, salacious piece of gossip that you can repeat and exaggerate? Do you search among the words you hear, looking for some subtle negative tone or nuance that you could take offence at? Some people spend their lives looking for things to be offended over, to the point where if they don't find it, they will make it up or twist what has been said in order to portray themselves as the victims.

It's a terrible way to live. I know, I've been there … but I'm not there any more.

Everything's always a drama for those people. Nothing is ever right. There's always something to complain about, someone or something to criticise, some innocent person's reputation to malign or destroy, some drama to be invented and maintained. There's always something to be offended about, some juicy morsel of self-pity or wounded pride or outraged dignity to share with friends. Many people strain to hear whatever can be misconstrued as hurtful or wrong to themselves or to people around them. They go looking for the negative.

That's why Jesus tells us to be very careful about what we *hear*.

People who are fluent in the language of life tend to go looking for life in all their conversations and they're more inclined to hear it as well as speak it. These are the people who often don't realise when someone is being sarcastic to them. They often don't pick up on hints or negative intimations or dubious sexual references. They've become so attuned to speaking life that they tend to hear life as well as speak it and often have to be told directly that someone was taking a sideswipe at them because they haven't realised it.

"The heart of the wise teaches his mouth and adds learning to his lips." (Proverbs 16:23)

Speaking life is not just about being positive, although optimism is a primary aspect of speaking life.

The words we speak ought to build and strengthen the people and situations around us, and sometimes that also means speaking correction that will help people recognise the wrong perspectives and attitudes that are destroying their lives. Life isn't always easy to speak because it often goes directly against the flow of the atmosphere it's surrounded by. There are times when it doesn't seem all that encouraging and at times it can be difficult to rake up the courage to speak life into a situation. Speaking life can be hugely challenging to the one who speaks it, as well the one who hears it.

Jesus commonly spoke to people about areas of their life that they hadn't realised were a problem. He did it with the rich young ruler, a guy who thought he was desperate for answers (Mark 10:21). As it turned out, he wasn't as desperate as he thought. The answer he got wasn't the answer he was looking for and he chose to walk away from Jesus rather than let those words of life change his life.

"Wounds from a friend are better than many kisses from an enemy." (Proverbs 27:6)

Sometimes only a friend who really loves you will have the courage and take the time to speak to you about the difficult things in your life – things you haven't noticed yourself. Those conversations can be the catalyst to change your life, helping you grow and develop as a person, if you're serious about hearing answers to your life's questions.

Or those same words of life may break the friendship, if you don't want to know.

The other problem is that sometimes we think we are speaking life when actually we are only speaking religious platitudes, rules and regulations, like the Pharisees. Religion only brings bondage and confusion. It's easier to follow a set of rules in many ways, because you don't have to maintain a relationship with Jesus Christ if you have a rulebook...

...but it also becomes impossible to speak life.

Jesus spoke life, not religion. Jesus made sense. People understood what He was on about.

Jesus had been healing loads of sick people and He'd just performed the miracle with the loaves and fish. The people were astonished at what was happening and they called Him a prophet. They crowded in on Him so much that He went up into the mountains for some time out and the disciples got into the boat to go to Capernaum. It was then that the storm hit and they were sure they would drown, until Jesus came walking out to them on the raging water and immediately they were through the hurricane and on the other side of the sea.

The crowd, who'd been fed miraculously with a kid's lunch, wanted to find Him. They knew He hadn't left in the boat, but when they realised He was on the other side, they crowded into other boats and followed Him, marvelling because they didn't know how He could possibly have got there.

Desperate for more miracles and craving for signs, they gathered around Him, expecting to see more astonishing things, but instead He began to speak to them at a whole new level. They sensed that something had changed, because previously He'd focused on their needs. But now the emphasis shifted and He began to tell them about what it would cost them if they truly wanted to follow Him. As He began to share the deep spiritual truths about where He came from and who He really was, they became antagonistic, pressing Him to explain what He was talking about. By the time He came to the point of telling them that they needed to eat His body and drink His blood, they were freaked out.

He was speaking life ... but it didn't sound like life to them.

It sounded like the ravings of a madman ... it sounded like blasphemy. They began to murmur among themselves and it wasn't life they were speaking, although I'm sure it sounded very reasonable at the time. And it wasn't only the crowd who were complaining. John says that many of Jesus' disciples, people who had followed Him closely up to now, were afraid and deeply disturbed (John 6:60). It was then that Jesus explained that the spiritual concepts He talked to them about are...

...life.

"The words that I have spoken to you are spirit and life." (John 6:63b)

A lot of people thought that was a bit too much and they turned and walked away, once and for all. Some of them were people who'd been following Him for a long time and who thought they knew Him well.

Words of life are spiritually discerned (1 Corinthians 2:14). The language of life is different from all other languages. Whenever and wherever it is spoken, it demands a response.

It challenges.

It strengthens.

It builds.

It establishes the purposes of God.

It divides between soul and spirit.

It affirms us and leads us to worship Him...

...but it's not an easy language to understand or to speak.
It's much easier to speak negativity, faithlessness, fear and doubt.

"So also, the tongue is a small thing, but what enormous damage it can do. A tiny spark can set a great forest on fire. And the tongue is a flame of fire. It is full of wickedness that can ruin your whole life. It can turn the entire course of your life into a blazing flame of destruction, for it is set on fire by hell itself." (James 3:5-6)

We cannot really comprehend the investment hell has made into stopping us, our family, our church and its members from going on any further in God's plan. It's vital to hell's mission that you personally are derailed from your destiny. The enemy's one plan is to destroy God's plan for your life, your family, your future, your nation. The weapons of his warfare may be the spears and arrows of fear, immorality, greed, shame or pride, but getting those emotions into your heart is often as simple as you or others speaking negatively over your life and the lives of those around you.

Check your tongue. Is it often critical, complaining, accusing, discouraging, sarcastic, impatient, negative... to yourself or others? If it is, you're speaking the native tongue of hell rather than the language of life. You need to shut the hell up. You can only do that by speaking life.

* * *

Among the greatest scourges of the Australian landscape are the bushfires that burn up huge tracts of land during the summer months, when thousands and even millions of acres are destroyed. These fires can be the result of one cigarette carelessly thrown onto the dry grass, or a piece of broken glass refracting the sun onto the brown foliage. However, it's shocking to know that in most cases the devastation is caused by arsonists deliberately setting fire to the bush.

Summer in Australia coincides with Christmas and it can be a traumatic time for the fire fighters. Working until they drop from exhaustion in the extreme heats of the summer and the fire combined, they don't get to spend Christmas with their families; they can't work at their jobs; they miss out on the holidays and some even lose their lives. Thousands of animals, many of them rare species threatened with extinction, are killed. Homes and livelihoods are lost, property and precious memories go up in smoke; insurance doesn't always cover the losses and families can be destroyed at times like this.

Many of the arsonists are immature and ignorant with no real idea of what they are doing. The Aussie authorities now take the culprits into the hospitals and animal shelters to stand face to face the results of their little prank, to see the truly catastrophic tragedies that have come out of their foolishness.

Our cultures are similarly spiritually blighted with drought, leaving them dry and flammable, ready to be destroyed by careless words and actions. God calls those who are willing to learn the language of life, as He did with Ezekiel, to gain His perspective and prophesy into the dryness and watch what He will do. As we call the things that are not as though they were, life surges forward.

Satan has no new ideas of his own. He is only able to copy what God has designed. We were designed to speak our world into being and Satan's determination is to influence our choice of words and attitudes in order to cause us to derail God's plan for our lives by the way we speak. We think we are just venting our frustration and disappointment. We don't realise how often we've struck a match that will end up burning away the hope and destiny that God has called us and others to. Our conversation affects our own lives as well as the lives of those around us. It affects our hopes and dreams.

Righteousness and love can so easily be destroyed by ignorant words. James emphasises this when he says: *"See how great a forest is set on fire by a little spark; the tongue is a fire..."* (James 3:5)

Fires roar through the Body of Christ, through churches and families and relationships when Christians unwittingly and thoughtlessly indulge their negativity by speaking out what the enemy wants us to see, rather than what God sees. If we could only see how tragically often God's purposes are thwarted because ordinary people unknowingly speak the language of hell, we would shut the hell up and change our language. Little fires, set alight by people who don't really mean any harm, but who don't understand the serious repercussions of what they are saying, can escalate problems and hurt until what started out as something relatively innocuous becomes catastrophic. Marriages are destroyed, businesses go under, nations fail and ministries implode – all because people who don't know any better are opening the situation up to hell's plans, rather than gaining God's perspective and speaking in a way that will shut hell down.

Most people have no idea they are committing arson in the Church. A restricted view of the vision of the Church makes it difficult to understand how a few little negative, critical or discouraging comments contribute to the overall pressure, and result in a lack of unity that often means God's hand of blessing is withheld. Every ministry effort becomes a hard slog, like pushing jelly uphill with your nose.

The Church is called to mission, to bring the life of Christ into a world that is parched and dry. Whether our words bring life or set a fire depends on our understanding of the impact of what we say. We need to learn how to counteract the prevailing atmosphere by speaking the language of life. The book of Proverbs tells us that the heart of the wise teaches their own mouth to speak. It's a symbiotic idea: the heart hears from God how He sees a particular thing and then the heart teaches the mouth to say what God says. The Kingdom of God is in our hearts and in our mouths.

"Being asked by the Pharisees when the kingdom of God would come, He answered them, 'The Kingdom of God is not coming with signs to be observed, nor will they say, "Look, here it is!" or "There!" for behold, the Kingdom of God is within you.'" (Luke 17:20-21)

Our future in Christ is amazing, wonderful, powerful, exhilarating and incredible. The purposes of God for His people are tangible and the Kingdom of God comes into view as His people speak it out and live it out. The Kingdom is so near us. It's in our heart and it's in our mouth. God equips us to co-labour with Him in transforming our families, our finances, our cities and nations, but we need to grasp that it begins with how we speak. He formed the world with His words and as people who are made in His image, we have the privilege and the responsibility to do the same thing.

The words we speak can be *spirit and life*, just like Jesus' words are. Or they can bring discouragement, humiliation, brokenness, shame and withdrawal. When you're discussing something, anything, remember to speak life.

It's too easy to indulge our own negativity by saying whatever we feel like. But if we are willing to learn to speak life, even when we don't feel like it, we will not only shut up the hell that is so rampant in our spheres of influence, but we will also find that we are collaborating with the Creator of the Universe to usher in His Kingdom.

9
You're In Charge Of Your Mouth

Decide to use your words as a vehicle for your faith

*"Notice the difference between what happens when
a man says to himself: 'I have failed three times'
and what happens when he says: 'I am a failure.'"*
~Hayakawa, S. I.

*"The tendency to whining and complaining may be taken as the
surest symptom of little souls and inferior intellects."*
~Lord Jeffrey

One of the greatest problems we have in the context of faith, prayer, and belief in God is the common misunderstanding that the roadblocks to living a life of faith come as a result of God saying no. We heard God (we thought), we've prayed, we've believed, and then we meet enough road blocks to eventually conclude that what we thought He said obviously was not what He actually said; or that maybe He did say it, but now He's changed His mind. In order to acquiesce to the roadblock, our mindsets need to accommodate the belief that God is schizophrenic, causing us to desire something and then making sure we don't have it.

Either that or people give up on God altogether and get on with trying to make a life without Him.

Good luck with that!

Accepting roadblocks as being from God, however, exposes an anomaly in our thinking. We heard from God, or we thought we did, and set about a course of action. We tried it; it didn't work. We tried again, harder this time; it still didn't work. If we're really, really determined we may try a few more times, but ultimately we give in, feeling confused and disappointed that God didn't show up and make it all come to pass like we thought He would.

Our view of God becomes increasingly constricted, conflicted and confined as we gradually accept in our hearts (though our minds may, for the rest of their lives, continue to repeat the lines they've been enculturised in) that God cannot be trusted to do for me what He says He will do. We have to conclude that it works for some people but not for everyone, and especially not for me.

Many people who come to this conclusion don't leave God or the Church (well, they may leave the Church). Instead, they settle for a lukewarm faith that is well meaning and righteous, but with no excitement, no exultant breakthroughs, no nerve wracking waits that tread the tightrope between absolute confidence and total failure, and consequently, no real, honest to goodness, mountain moving, exhilarating faith-filled faith.

What you settle for is where you'll live.

"I know your works as well as your labour and steadfast endurance, and that you cannot tolerate evil. You have even put to the test those who refer to themselves as apostles (but are not), and have discovered that they are false. I am also aware that you have persisted steadfastly, endured much for the sake of my name, and have not grown weary. But I have this against you: you have departed from your first love! Therefore, remember from what high state you have fallen, and repent!" (Revelation 2:2-5)

First love isn't the love we had initially, because in human terms, most people begin with strong attraction and, as the relationship grows, the love grows too. Many older married couples love each other far more deeply and passionately after years of being together than they did in the early years. The reason for that is their determination to stay in love even when they don't always feel like it. Youth doesn't have exclusive rights to fervour and depth of love.

Rather, the first love referred to here is the deliberate choice to make passion for Christ preeminent, so that no other love can overrule it. It means putting Jesus first in the way we live our lives; it means seeking the Kingdom of God first.

It's not only possible, but also very common to live a Christian life that is patient, hard working, merciful, persistent and faithful, but with no blaze of fervent expectation that stems from a deep and passionate love affair with Him. Even the most enthusiastic, passionate Christian life can easily devolve into a steady, trudging, dutiful service in which our need for security and comfortable predictability overrules the pressures and avoids the risks that a passionate, faith-filled life accepts as the norm.

Sensible Christianity spells death to faith-filled faith.

Despite opinions to the contrary, real faith is not easy or safe. People who are deeply in love, as John hears spoken of regarding the Church in Ephesus, gain their security from their innate awareness of how the other party will act towards them, even in times of trouble or insecurity. Love then becomes something more than whether we remain sensible or steady, and more than whether we got our needs met, moving into an entirely different dimension where faith is a combination of total trust in the One who calls you, and a wild free fall that converts our feeble footsteps into the soaring of eagle's wings.

It's about trust...

...and trust arises out of a deep understanding of the other person's character.

"God is good, all the time," we say, but we don't always believe that. We can't understand why He allows bad things to happen to good people and, for that matter, why He allows good things to happen to bad people. We worship and praise Him, pray and serve Him, but when the chips are down and we suffer loss, it is easier to think He has let us down because He doesn't care, than to think that there may be more to the situation than meets the eye.

That's because even though we love Him, we don't really know Him all that well. We don't know Him well enough to trust Him. Real faith recognises that there's more to the story than the facts suggest. If He promised to provide all our needs, and right now we have unmet needs, it's worth looking into the surrounding circumstances. Sometimes change is required, but sometimes it's a matter of holding on in faith until there's a breakthrough.

Fight the good fight of faith to which you were called (1 Timothy 6:12). Faith is always a fight. In fact, we could go so far as to say that if it doesn't involve a fight, it's not faith. We are always at war against an enemy who wants to kill us, steal from us, and destroy our lives, our faith and our effectiveness for God (John 10:10).

Fighting spiritually is very different from fighting physically. I've observed that many of the physically and intellectually strongest people I know are those who are least inclined to learn how to fight in faith. Maybe it's because they have learned to rely on their own muscles or intellect and don't want to engage with the trade off required to learn how to fight in the supernatural realm, where brains and physical strength don't rule. It takes a special sort of understanding to get out into the deep waters of faith without a paddle...

...or a canoe.

The more we know the character of God, the greater our strength to fight in the supernatural realms of faith. Most of the times when we meet resistance as we pursue God's purposes, it's not God who's saying no.

So, if it's not God saying no ... don't take NO for an answer! Let me say that again in another way. When God puts something into your heart and you meet resistance, it's not God who's saying no. If you can grasp that, your capacity to stand against rulers of wickedness in high places (Ephesians 6:12) will increase greatly. Those rulers of wickedness are just as determined to thwart the purposes of God operating in and through your life as God is to see them established.

We've got to choose sides, but often we don't realise that it's our conversation that illustrates most profoundly whose side we're on. Revelation of the character of God is the key component for success in any faith fight. Get to know Him, because the more you know Him, the greater understanding you will have of who it is that is hindering, blocking and attempting to stop you as you work towards the establishment of the Kingdom of God in your sphere of influence.

If it's not God saying no, don't take no for an answer. The only way we can know the difference is through our revelation of what God has said and our determination to believe that to be true, despite whatever facts are laid out in front of us. You see, the facts are not the truth, and an effective walk of faith is contingent on whether we really know that.

If you believe the facts rather than God's word, you are beaten before you start. Does that mean you deny the facts and pretend they don't exist? That's the take that some people have on faith, but honestly, that can't be the answer. If you operate in denial, people will think you're deluded and that you haven't been taking your meds. And that may be true.

Remember Abraham didn't say he wasn't old, he just made a decision to allow himself to be called the "father of nations". David didn't say Goliath was a pipsqueak; on the contrary, he knew he was up against a giant. But he also had the revelation of who God was in him. He'd had his courage developed during his days in the field; his skill sets had been sharpened as he practised with his weapon of choice, the slingshot. But beyond that was something greater: he had revelation of the power of God as it operates through the believer against whatever threat arises. Goliath had risen against Israel, but David was ready for him.

Being ready is key. It's too late to get ready when the problem occurs. Readiness takes place in the boring, quiet times – the times when no one, including you, is even aware that you're being prepared. Readiness comes by treating every situation and every mundane choice as though it was important; as though it had the power to change you to become more like the person God ordained you to be – which it does.

Readiness develops when you take each tiny temptation to fear or pretence or retaliation or lack of integrity, and use it to help you change. Maturity of faith means that who you are has changed so that the light of Christ can shine more powerfully out of your life. Your reactions are different to society's general responses and people can see that. Your choices have changed and whether people comment on it or not, they realise you are not who you were, and you're not who other people are either. The more you change, the more others see that you love and serve God, whether they would say it that way or not.

This is how you develop when you refuse to let a crowd mentality force you into a mould, but rather choose to do what God wants you to do, even though it's inconvenient or embarrassing or it means you lose street cred with some of your friends. If what you're doing is not the done thing in your circle, maybe your circle needs to change – either by them seeing what you are becoming and wanting that for themselves, or by you or them voting with their feet. Some friendships won't last the test of the changes that are taking place in you as you become more like Jesus, and that's the truth.

That is hard to accept, especially when you've been in a relationship for a long time, but something that is not often preached is that Jesus didn't come to bring peace on earth but a sword that would divide people. Even the closest of relationships can find it difficult when one chooses to walk a life of radical faith and the other doesn't.

Don't be rejected; it's not really about you. It's between them and God.

Negatives develop in the dark. Speaking life is an irritant to people who want to hug their negativity close to their chest and nurse it in their heart. Negativity is habit forming and addictive and it's impossible to go cold turkey, but anyone can ask God to help them train their mouth and heart to speak differently. Just as with other addictions, when you begin to speak a Kingdom message, some of the people around you who are addicted to negativity will find it so challenging that they will mock you, criticising and deriding your new way of speaking. In the end, the challenge rests on who you are following, who you believe, and who you want to become.

God is not a schoolmaster standing with a stick in His hand, waiting to see if you can make the grade. God wants to bless you. He wants to direct your life and take you on mind boggling adventures of faith. He wants you to succeed in the plan He has for you. Sometimes faith is just pure, dogged determination to do what you know God has said, despite all evidence to the contrary. The capacity to do that grows in us as we grow in Him.

That's all there is to it!

Simple!

10
The Word
@ Work

Make sure that what you are saying is what you want to reap

"*There is always one moment in childhood when the door opens and lets the future in.*"
~Graham Greene

"*The inner speech, your thoughts, can cause you to be rich or poor, loved or unloved, happy or unhappy, attractive or unattractive, powerful or weak.*"
~Ralph Charell

Is it nature or nurture that predominantly moulds and forms a person into their eventual shape and causes their destiny to be set in stone? Are you the way you are because of some curiously random and fickle combination of good and bad traits inherited from your forebears? Or would you have been pretty near perfect had it not been for the complex negative effects of the environment you were raised in – an environment over which you had no control? The answer is yes ... and no, because there is more to the process of becoming who we are than the complexity of our DNA combined with the culture and environment we were raised in.

Ultimately, no matter how difficult life is, we must all take responsibility for the person we end up becoming.

We are formed by God, influenced and impacted by our environment. But ultimately, we are shaped by our choices. Our gifts, talents and skill sets are inherently built into our DNA. The subtle alchemy of genetic inheritance, combined with the call of God, conspired to design us even before we were formed in the womb.

God created Jeremiah to be His voice to the nation of Israel before Jeremiah had even been conceived. Believe it or not, He does the same with us. However, from very early on, circumstances and surroundings connive to sow all sorts of seeds – the good, the bad and the ugly – into the field that will become our identity. All these seeds grow together like the wheat and the weeds Jesus talked of (Matthew 13:25), until ultimately the decisions we make concerning what has been sown into our lives by others and ourselves will dictate what kind of crop our field will produce.

Will my identity and destiny be expressed by the wheat or the weeds?

All babies are beautiful, and very few people intentionally do anything to damage an infant's life. However, despite everyone's good intentions, *rejection*, the most common of all the negative emotions experienced since Eden, starts very early. Children get no say in what parents, siblings, teachers and strangers sow into their lives. That's why it's not long before briars and thorns take root in our psyche and our behaviour begins to express the degree to which our lives have become subject to the words that have spiked, torn and wounded our hearts – sometimes by those who loved us first, as well as those who love us most.

Angry, impatient, insulting words, and cruel, careless jokes can mar a person's life forever. I've never met a person who couldn't recount in detail events in which certain identity-defining words were spoken to them in their early years. Those words can be counted on to reaffirm their worthlessness whenever circumstances and pain press the replay button. Without Christ, no one, no matter how famous or celebrated, feared or respected, can escape the cruel inner testimony that drives us to perform and seeks to prove to us once and for all how woefully inadequate we really are. Despite their blatant lack of subtlety, those inner words are the most finely honed and intense form of torture, because they find their way into the deepest and most vulnerable places of our heart instantly and without hesitation. The reason they are able to do this is because we can't help but agree, regardless of our most determined efforts to prove the contrary.

Some of the greatest business, political, church and corporate leaders who have clawed their way to the top in an effort to prove that inner voice wrong, have found that despite their best efforts, those words continue to rise up when least expected, turning every success to ashes and magnifying every loss out of all proportion. There is only one answer and you have to be in relationship with the Creator in order to even access it. The decision to change your perspective to something beyond that which your history dictates about you requires undertaking the world's longest and most important journey: that of your head to your heart. You've got to change the seeds you sow.

"Do not be deceived; God is not mocked, for whatever one sows, that will he also reap. For the one who sows to his own flesh will from the flesh reap corruption, but the one who sows to the Spirit will from the Spirit reap eternal life." (Galatians 6:7-8)

* * *

In the days before automated agriculture, farmers sowed their fields by hand. The menial task of trudging up and down the lines that had already been prepared to receive the seed required no particular thought. The sower need only pace mindlessly along the track, allowing the seeds to pour like liquid out of her hands into the waiting furrows.

Thoughts and speech operate in much the same way. Our brains have developed ruts in which well worn attitudes and thought patterns have made it easy for us to live and relate without thinking any new thoughts or challenging the old ones we've lived with for so long. We continue to pour out the well worn words or jokes or warnings or opinions as seeds into our own lives and the lives of others, without knowing whether those words still fit (if indeed they ever did). Society is filled with people who were told they'd never amount to anything, and some of them didn't, but there are people who escaped the trap their history set for them because one day they made the decision to get out of the rut of thought patterns they'd inherited from someone else in order to take on board God's opinion of them.

"For as the rain and the snow come down from heaven and do not return there, but water the earth, making it bring forth and sprout, giving seed to the sower and bread to the eater, so shall my word that goes out from my mouth; it shall not return to me empty, but it shall accomplish that which I purpose, and shall succeed in the thing for which I sent it. For you shall go out in joy and be led forth in peace; the mountains and the hills before you shall break forth into singing and all the trees of the field shall clap their hands. Instead of the briar shall come up the myrtle; and it shall make a name for the Lord, an everlasting sign that shall not be cut off." (Isaiah 55:10–13)

It's a scary thought, but the seeds that have been allowed to take root in your life are very easily identifiable. Fear, kindness, generosity, anger, bitterness, purity, rage, unbelief, encouragement, self pity, courage, lust, shame, selfishness, apathy – regardless of what the seed is, it multiplies rapidly once the roots have gained a foothold. People don't always see what is being sown at the time of sowing, but it doesn't take long for them to see what is growing in your life.

Isaiah's description of the effectiveness of God's word to change lives is startling for people who feel as though their lives are full of briars and thorns. He speaks about how God's word is able to bring fruitfulness and success and peace and joy, and in verse 13 promises that if people can grasp this reality, the briars in our lives will be replaced with myrtle trees.

Myrtle is a really interesting choice for several reasons. The blossoms of the myrtle are highly fragrant, which speaks of the fragrance of Christ. But myrtle also apparently has the capacity to express its entire history through its trunk. Where it is planted and what has taken place around it will show on the streaks of colour in its timber, the shape of the beautiful burls on its trunk, etc. The tree converts its entire history, whether good or bad, harsh or serene, into a unique expression of growth and beauty. Like Myrtle trees, we have the capacity to take all that has happened to us and use them in such a way that we grow to become strong and lovely, despite our wounds and scars. Wherever we go, the perfume of Christ can be an alluring fragrance, drawing others to Him as it surrounds our lives.

"Listen! A sower went out to sow. And as he sowed, some seed fell along the path and the birds came and devoured it. Other seed fell on rocky ground, where it did not have much soil, and immediately it sprang up, since it had no depth of soil. And when the sun rose it was scorched, and since it had no root, it withered away. Other seed fell among the thorns and the thorns grew up and choked it, and it yielded no grain. And other seeds fell into good soil and produced grain, growing up and increasing and yielding thirtyfold and sixtyfold and a hundredfold ...

...The sower sows the word. And these are the ones along the path, where the word is sown; when they hear, Satan immediately comes and takes away the word that is sown in them. And these are the ones sown on rocky ground; the ones who, when they hear the word, immediately receive it with joy. And they have no root in themselves but endure for a while; then, when tribulation or persecution arises on account of the word, immediately they fall away. And others are the ones sown among thorns.

They are those who hear the word, but the cares of the world and the deceitfulness of riches and the desires for other things enter in and choke the word and it proves unfruitful. But those that were sown on the good soil are the ones who hear the word and accept it and bear fruit, thirtyfold and sixtyfold and a hundredfold." (Mark 4:3-8, 14-20)

We are the soil, but we are the sower also. We are not only subject to the things that are said to us, we also customarily speak to ourselves about ourselves and our world in a way that sows the seeds for our future life. We are influenced by what other people say and we influence ourselves as well – and then we act accordingly.

Imagine you're the field and you're the farmer as well. You have made the decision to get rid of the weeds that have been choking the field and strangling the good seed. You start scattering good seed, godly values, thoughts, attitudes and actions; you make a decision to be honest and pure with your decisions.

When seed is sown the field is then fertilised to promote a healthy and strong harvest.

When people start making deliberate choices to really live like a Christian, they always get fertilised.

Have you ever been near a farm that's just been fertilised? It stinks for miles around. People wrinkle their noses and make a few choice remarks, especially if they don't realise that what they can smell is fertiliser.

As the sower and the field, what does fertilisation look like for you? Despite all your great intentions, all the good decisions you've made, it feels like all you get back is crap! Seriously! Nothing's working!

People misunderstand and misrepresent you. You tell the truth and you get the sack from your job. You decide to give more financially and you get more bills. You do the right thing and get the wrong result. Parts of your life begin to stink ... that's the fertiliser! And regardless of how it feels, you need it so that the good seed you've been sowing can grow!

God has to train us how to do war in spiritual realms (Psalm 18:34). We'd never learn how to fight unless we had something to fight against, but instead of learning how to pray and speak in order to change the atmosphere and get the breakthrough, we become afraid or irritated or offended with God and we stop praying and begin to look for our own solution. It's always hard to push through and the ever-present temptation is to stop pushing! Don't stop pushing because it isn't working yet. It's like pushing a huge boulder; it takes a while to get the momentum. But once you get it rolling, it will keep going for a long time, even after you stop pushing. Sometimes it takes a while to build momentum in prayer and speaking life, but don't stop. Keep pushing; it will come.

"And let us not grow weary of doing good, for in due season we will reap, if we do not give up." (Galatians 6:9)

It's worth the cost to plant and then nurture good seed, despite the hardships that you experience in the process. If you are willing to see it through, you will reap a harvest.

* * *

Once fertiliser is spread on a field it must be watered thoroughly and regularly to dissolve it. If this doesn't happen, the seedlings will be so badly burned they'll be destroyed. It's the watering that transforms fertiliser into the catalyst for the growth of your harvest, rather than act as the agent of death to your newly developing faith. It's vital that the seeds you planted and the fertiliser that now surrounds them are watered regularly from the word of God.

We begin our journey of faith just wanting to please God and prove that His word works miracles. Instead of success, we find an avalanche of crap has been triggered and is rapidly spreading all over our good intentions. You exercised faith but the reverse of what you believed for happened. You acted in kindness and you got misunderstood. You gave generously and people used you!

It's at this point that you need to remember why you are doing what you are doing. Remember, it was God who called you. Remember the importance of what He directed you to do. Remember His word and say it to your circumstances, just like Jesus did in that wilderness place when the devil was tempting Him and His life seemed barren and dry and hungry.

The most faith filled people have times when it doesn't look like God is working on their behalf. At these times we feel bare and exposed to the elements of our circumstances and the ridicule of the onlookers. This is the time when giving up looks like a pretty good option. No matter how used you are to living in faith, you always hit times when what you are doing appears to be absolutely wacky.

Three times in the New Testament we are told that the righteous live by their faith (Romans 1:17, Galatians 3:11, Hebrews 10:38). Only faith can train you to speak the word of God over a rubbish day. Only faith can get you through the times when imminent disaster looms. Get familiar with your Bible. When you see things in there that run counter to what you are experiencing, use it as a learning opportunity to sow that word out as water over your circumstances. Your circumstances will change if you don't give up.

You're exhausted and feel overwhelmed: I can do all things through Christ who strengthens me.

You've given more than you can afford and you're not sure if your money will last through the month: My God shall supply all my need according to His riches in glory by Christ Jesus. (This scripture relates to the earlier part of the chapter – it's a promise made as a result of the giving of the people whose need God is now promising to supply.)

You have been misjudged and people are speaking badly about you: Isaiah 54:17 says, No weapon formed against me shall prosper and every tongue that raises itself against me, I rebuke. God will vindicate me because I'm serving Him.

If you just resign yourself to the crap that's spreading out all over the field that you've sown in faith, your faith will be burned and maybe even destroyed.

Fertiliser demands a response! You get to decide if it's a godly response. It's a two-part exercise. You don't just do the right thing and wait for God to make everything work for you. You take into account that crap is going to come your way and you make the choice to use it as fertiliser for the good life you've chosen to live instead of letting it destroy that life.

You water your seed AND the fertiliser with God's word. That's how you get beautiful, strong, sweet smelling trees in what used to be a patch of briars and thorns. It requires a deliberate decision to do something beyond what is a natural response. The reason why the faith of many Christians is weakened and feeble is because after they've sown their seed they wait passively for something to happen and then they're disillusioned and disappointed when they only get crap. They forget that you need manure to fertilise seed if you want a strong and fruitful harvest.

"Those who plant in tears will harvest with shouts of joy. They weep as they go to plant their seed, but they sing as they return with the harvest." (Psalm 126:5-6)

Turn the crap into fertiliser! Make it work for you! The God who has called you is faithful to make your life work (1 Thessalonians 5:24), but it requires co-labouring with Him, as opposed to lying back and letting Him get on with it. It's true that there are tears in the planting, but it doesn't have to end there. It's supposed to end with a party, a time of singing and rejoicing.

When God's word is spoken out, it literally rains on what has been sown and can eventually replace all the harsh and hurtful things that have been said and done. It's a miracle and no one knows how it happens. Regardless of what happened to you when you were young, as time goes on the responsibility for what is growing in you becomes your own. Maturity in Christ always shows itself as sweet smelling trees instead of briars.

11
Don't Take *No* For An Answer

Knowing when it's not God who's saying NO

"'Come to the edge,' he said. They said: 'We are afraid.' 'Come to the edge,' he said. They came. He pushed them and they flew!"
~Guillaume Apollinaire

"There are dreamers, but not all human beings dream equally. Some are dreamers of the night, who in the dusty recesses of their mind dream and wake in the morning to find it was just vanity, but the Dreamers of the Day are dangerous people, for they may act their dream with open eyes, and make it possible."
~T.E. Lawrence

There's no purpose in making a point unless you can back it up. Speaking life is a fantastic tool to enable faith to rise and soar through the average and beyond the mediocre into the wild blue yonder of awesome events. Through it we can live a life less ordinary, in contrast to what much of the Church and the watching world have come to view as normal Christianity.

Faith, like any other Christian value, develops in stages; from glory to glory, strength to strength, challenge to challenge and breakthrough to breakthrough. We are changed by degrees (2 Corinthians 3:18), beginning with small experiments in faith and growing from there.

Speaking life carries an enormous power to change our circumstances, with maturity in this language developing in stages. It begins with the small steps of speaking life into your own environment, your own bills, relationships, health and circumstances. Success breeds success. When you see God at work in the small things, it's easier to believe for greater things, graduating even to impossible things.

I include in this chapter the stories of a number of life-speakers, at different stages of becoming fluent in the language of life. The stories may not appear to be world changing, but the beginnings we make in the walk of faith is what causes our faith muscles to build and go from strength to strength. The more breakthroughs we see in our present circumstances, the stronger will be our position to believe for breakthrough in the next arena.

The following are some amazing, true accounts of that have happened to Rick and me, or to people we know personally. I promise you that these stories are not exaggerated or evang-elastic, but are verifiable by those who saw them happen and by the official evidence that supports them. They are stories of ordinary people who had the courage to experiment with speaking life into their own version of dry bones. To their astonishment, and that of lots of other people too, they saw life springing out of hopeless situations.

Orkney Or Bust! – Bev Murrill

It was Friday 23rd June, 1999 and we were on the way to the Orkney Islands for a conference – twelve women on a fourteen seater bus. We had left just before midnight, giving ourselves 18 hours to drive from Essex to Scrabster at the tip of Scotland to catch the 6:00pm ferry, which would get us to the conference centre in time for the first meeting at 8:00pm. It was CGC Orkney's first women's conference on an island where women's conferences were not common and, coincidentally, there was a white witch wedding being held there on the same night. The other key speaker and myself were on the bus and everyone was excited.

By 6:00am we were on the M6 near Preston and only the driver and her front passenger were awake, when suddenly a semitrailer lorry travelling just in front of us lost control. Fortunately, our driver and the car next to us were able to stop in time as the lorry turned first on its side and then skewed violently across the road, ending up with its wheels facing us as it blocked the entire road from the median strip to the grass verge.

The police arrived almost instantly and we ladies sat with our cups of tea observing the proceedings while the early morning traffic began to build up behind us. At 6:45am the police informed us that we would not be moving until 2:00pm as the truck was full of peaches and needed to be unloaded before it could be turned up the right way so that the road could be cleared.

Consternation in our little camp! With an 18-hour travel time we knew we could comfortably be at the ferry in time, but now 7 hours had been snatched from us. How could we get to the conference in time for the start? We had absolutely no chance if we missed that ferry; there wasn't another till the next day.

We began to pray, as did CGC Orkney and CGC Chelmsford. As the bus filled with the sound of women taking authority over the powers of darkness that wanted to prevent us from getting there, and speaking out our faith that the God who called us would be faithful to bring us to that ferry on time (1 Thessalonians 5:24), an idea occurred to me. Getting out of the bus, I went to the police officer in charge and suggested to him that they get an angle grinder and cut a gap through the metal-encased concrete barrier between our side and the other side of the highway. That way everyone could drive over the grass in the middle and turn back the other way to find a detour. Needless to say, the officer wasn't impressed with my suggestion and when I pushed the point he firmly said, "Madam, please return to your vehicle," which I did...

But we continued to pray and speak out the breakthrough we knew was ours. There's nothing that can rattle the powers of darkness like a group of women reinforcing God's unshakeable plan. We had a ferry to catch and a conference to do! And now those cups of tea were beginning to work their way through our systems and there were not only no toilets in the bushes, but there weren't any bushes ... for miles around there was only green grass ... and the jam of trucks and vans behind us ensured that we twelve ladies would have no privacy to answer the call of nature! Surprising what God uses to motivate you at times, isn't it.

As we prayed and spoke out in faith that we would be catching that 6:00pm ferry, it occurred to us to pray that God would send an older police officer to the scene, one who would have the power to make whatever bizarre decisions might be required to get us out of there. Amazingly, just as we spoke it, a man looked in the window to reassure us. Yep, grey hair and a few wrinkles ... he was old enough. Getting out of the bus again, I approached him with the same idea – how about getting an angle grinder to cut through the barrier so that we could drive over and go back the other way? His response was similar to the other guy, ending with me getting back into the bus...

But ignominy and faith are mutually exclusive. When you've got a cause and you know that God is at work, embarrassment doesn't get much of a look in. We knew that God had called us to Orkney at that particular time and that the situation we were facing was not from Him. That gave us courage and determination to keep praying and speaking out that we would be on that ferry at 6.00pm that night. We refused to take no for an answer...

... and as we prayed...

... we heard the sound of the angle grinder cutting through the barrier.

Those metal barriers are filled with concrete to stop cars breaking through them if there's an accident on the highway. They were so heavy that each short piece of steel-encased concrete took two police officers to carry them out of the way. Very soon, however, there was enough space for a small van to fit through. One of the ladies, Ali Tulloch, who was making conversation with the truck drivers, reported that all up and down the line of traffic the truckers were on their CB radios saying, "They're cutting the median barrier for that group of women in the bus." No one had ever heard of anything like that before ... or since, apparently.

Ours was the first vehicle over and at 7:20am we were driving back to a nearby roadside service station where everyone was able to relieve themselves of their cuppa and get another one. Another car had followed us and we heard from him that after us, only he and one other van had been allowed to cross. The police had then stopped the great escape, saying the ground was too soft to carry the weight. When we passed back the same way on Monday, no evidence of the median barrier being cut remained. The fence had been repaired as though it never happened.

But it did happen. God honoured our faith in the impossible because "faith is the substance of the things that you hope for, and the evidence of the things that you don't see." (Hebrews 11:1). Our hope was to go to Orkney and bring a message of the love of Jesus Christ for the women of that beautiful island and we had decided not to take no for an answer.

And as it turned out ... the answer wasn't NO. It was a yes from us and a great big YES from God.

Nitrous – Skye Doel

We're a doggy family. We love our dogs; they're part of the family. My husband Matt and I owned a boxer called Nitrous who, at the time, was the love of our lives. One day he got out onto the road and was hit by a car. The vet said he had no chance of survival as he'd broken so many bones, but we refused to take no for an answer. We prayed over him, cared for him, and continually spoke out words of faith in God for his healing and restoration. Slowly, and to everyone's amazement, including us and especially the vet, Nitrous recovered. You don't have to take no for an answer. God cares about what matters to you.

School days – Nicky Everett

I have worked with some challenging children in my teaching career and have always felt totally in control. I could pretty much handle whatever they threw at me. Then Jack (not his real name) joined our school. Jack was a 4-year old boy with some serious special needs. We didn't know that when he arrived, since his parents refused to acknowledge there was any kind of problem, despite the fact that it was clear even to an outsider that the family were in crisis management mode. With two small, demanding boys needing a lot of attention, mum was near burnout and close to an emotional breakdown. Dad was the breadwinner, the one holding it all together, the one the boys would listen to and the one mum leaned on. As long as he kept all these pieces together, there wasn't a problem.

In school, we saw a very different child to the one they knew at home. Jack was an isolated child who didn't have many friends and was fiercely independent. We soon learned that he liked to have everything his own way. If a child he wanted to play with was playing with another child, he would fly into an uncontrollable rage, biting the other child and throwing toys and furniture around the classroom. Nothing we tried made a difference and after a few weeks of trying to manage this destructive behaviour, using all the positive strategies recommended by educational professionals and working closely with parents, the staff in my school were literally on their knees and looking to me as head teacher to find a solution.

I tried everything I could think of: a firm approach, a creative strategy, reward charts, adult 1 to 1 time, time in the classroom, time out of the classroom, working with parents, the list felt endless, but nothing worked and his behaviour deteriorated as his frustration and ours grew. Children in the class were scared of him; parents were complaining and removing their children from our school. The whole situation felt like a train crash and I was the one who was supposed to be in control. I felt useless and my perception was that everyone was judging me as useless because my hands were tied. The Local Authority would not help; his case was not serious enough I was told; the parents told us it was our problem and we had to deal with it. Everyday I went to school with a heavy heart and increasing sense of desperation.

The situation came to a head one grey Tuesday, when Jack was having one of his tantrums and the support assistant restrained him and brought him out of the classroom as the focus of his tantrum was aimed at one of the other children. As she walked with him across the hall, he turned, kicked her and pushed her leg from under her to trip her up. She fell to the floor, crashing on her face as she used her hands to push him out of the way so she didn't fall onto him and hurt him. As a result she smashed her glasses, which cut her face, and had two black eyes. The fall resulted in a trip to the hospital and letters from her family citing legal action if she was hurt again because of his behaviour. Again, no one would listen and offer us support. The only option I felt was to manage him myself. I cleared my diary so that if he had a tantrum, I would manage it. Within a week, I had restrained him more times that I care to remember, had bruises up and down my legs where he had looked me in the face and kicked me, I had been scratched, punched, bitten, and spat at. My staff was grateful that they no longer had to manage him, but this was not a long term answer.

I remember that time as being at rock bottom. I was a new headteacher and believed that God had clearly called me to that position. I felt like a failure and the school was unravelling as all of my time and attention was focused on one child. How could one four-year-old child beat me? I could easily spend three hours a day just holding him tight and calming him down and my work was piling up around me.

In church, Bev was preaching on the authority of praying in Jesus' name and at the end of the meeting I spent some time talking to her about the problems I was facing in school. She taught me how to pray into this situation. It sounded ridiculous as I have been a Christian for 20 odd years and I knew how to pray! But she taught me word by word how to pray for this specific situation, calling on Jesus' name to take authority over it, the spiritual atmosphere in school, and to name very specifically the things I was standing against, such as rebellion and frustration. Furthermore, she also taught me how to edify and build myself up by praying in tongues to give me all the resources and strength I needed to cope. I made a promise to myself that I would pray exactly how she had taught me every day on the way to work, and so I did just that.

I would like to say that miraculously the situation changed overnight. It didn't and I still had to endure the kicks, punches and bites. But gradually, over a period of a month or so, the spiritual atmosphere changed in school. I found that when Jack was so angry that he was red and hitting out at everything and everyone, I had the strength to hold him, praying in tongues over him quietly until he calmed. What was more interesting was that staff was released from the bitterness and fear of this child and we began to talk about it as a team. Rather than the accusatory tones and frustration that were formerly used, we found we could speak positively and recognise the needs of this hurting child and his family. The situation finally ended for us when he was moved by the Local Authority to specialist provision. It took us nine months to fight for the placement he needed and I hear that he is now doing brilliantly.

Hard as it was, this situation taught me how to pray effectively for the first time. I take authority over the spiritual atmosphere every day now in my school, speaking life into it and I know it works. I have seen and felt the difference. I believe my school belongs to God and this is one of the tools He has given me to enable me to be a leader in that place.

The New House - Rick and Bev Murrill
When the recession hit the UK in 2008, it hit us too. We had sold our home for a good price and, in an attempt to generate more

funds for Cherish Uganda, our village for children with AIDs (www.
cherishuganda.org), we had invested the money in a company
which dealt in property. However, circumstances caused that
business to fail, and when it went down, so did we!

We had purchased a tiny terraced house with the intention of doing
it up and selling it on, but our changed circumstances meant we
needed to live in it ourselves. Aussies tend to live in houses that are
spacious with lots of room to entertain people – everything that
this little house wasn't. We appreciated that we had somewhere to
live, but as the months went on, we began to chafe against the fact
that we could only ever have two people around to visit at a time.
We were heartbroken that our former family events were now
impossible and we came to realise that though God had provided
a place for us to go, it wasn't where He intended us to stay. We
began to think about what we wanted in our next house and we
asked the Lord to provide for us a four bedroom house with plenty
of room upstairs and down for guests, visitors and our family. We
asked for conservatory, a dining room and a utility room, as well as
a workshop for Rick.

Praying together as a married couple is not an easy habit to get
into it, but it's definitely worth the effort. Because we're now in
the habit, we prayed together most days and we would thank the
Lord for our four-bedroom house with its workshop, conservatory,
dining room and utility room. We spoke out what we needed as
opposed to what we thought we could afford. We didn't complicate
the matter by telling the Lord how and why He would not be able
to give it to us. We had asked Him for it and now we were thanking
Him and trusting that He had the ability to sort out how to make it
happen.

We prayed and looked for a house, finding the perfect one quite quickly. It needed renovation, but it was in good condition and had four bedrooms, a dining room, conservatory, huge utility room AND a workshop! Fantastic! So far so good! However, we had an added complication: because Rick was in his mid-sixties, there were only two lending institutions that would consider giving us a mortgage.

The house was empty, so we made a deal with the owner that we could move in and rent until our mortgage came through. We moved in late August 2010 and two weeks later we went on a ministry trip to the USA. While we were there, we heard from the first lender that our application had been turned down.

It's important to say that this is not something we would advise anyone to do, and the reason we did it was only because we knew that God had guided us this way. For that reason, even though both of us admitted to one night each in which we found it difficult to sleep, for the most part our faith didn't waver. We also made the decision to tell very few people the situation we were in. At times like this, anyone who is not used to getting God's perspective and walking by faith would have very strong opinions over what we were doing and they wouldn't hesitate to express them. We couldn't afford their words of death to go out into the spiritual atmosphere over our faith battle. We knew that, naturally speaking, what we had done was not normal or sensible, in fact it was downright madness, but we also knew that God was in it. We asked for prayer from a very few folk whom we could trust to suspend their own disbelief and pray in faith for us. This is one of the biggest keys to operating in faith. Don't allow people, no matter how much they love you, to speak into your situation if they are not people of faith and if they don't understand the concept of speaking life. Sometimes that may mean not talking about it to too many people.

The following week we had news that the second lending body had given us the mortgage, no questions asked. In addition, we were £10,000 short in the money that was required, but we also knew that God was not going to let us down at this point. Right in the nick of time, just as all the paperwork was going through, we received a gift of that amount from a woman who valued us as people. God had moved her heart to bless us … and we had ourselves a house.

It's worth training yourself to believe God instead of the facts. We couldn't have believed for our house if we hadn't learned in earlier days to believe for electricity bills to be paid, cars to be provided, even holidays for our family. Don't start your speaking life journey with something so huge that you'll fall in a heap if you fail. Begin where you are and let God take you on a journey to some of the most amazing examples of His provision. Some people won't believe what God has done for you. That's okay. It doesn't matter what people think; it only matters what God thinks.

Personal testimony – Anonymous

I have always fought against the negative effects of my past. I was very messed up, with awful coping mechanisms, but if I hadn't been as stubborn as I was – determined that I was strong and wouldn't allow anyone to destroy me – I would probably have been in a much worse state. I had a long history of being withdrawn but showing reckless behaviour at times and made several suicide attempts. I was constantly torn between who I was and who I dreamt of being, with mental battles tearing me apart every waking minute. I tried to keep my head above water.

I threw myself into church, I always kept my faith, I had treatment for mental health problems in hospital, and I received secular and Christian counselling. I made myself accountable by meeting people for prayer and I read lots of books to attain my ever elusive healing.

It all played its part and I did improve a lot. I even managed to work at a healthy marriage and became a doting mum ... but rubbish kept rearing its head and there was always something missing. None of it hit that deepest, darkest point of shame, guilt, depression and self-loathing that I hid so well.

Then I moved church to CGC Chelmsford. It was a new place and not many people knew my background or me, so I tried even harder to hide everything I was, pretending to be the person I wanted to be. But it wasn't real and I still hurt. When I first came to CGC I was suffering from bulimia with anorexic tendencies. I was making myself sick 5 or 6 times a day and sometimes more, starving myself when I thought I was too heavy. I was still self-harming, wearing long enough sleeves to hide the cuts on my arms. I was taking antidepressants and suffering from anxiety disorder, often having to plan my escape route at church in case the noise and people overwhelmed me. I was having panic attacks and couldn't let my guard down in front of these people I valued as new friends. I couldn't let them see I was screwed up. I was invited to BE 2009, a women's conference, and I was a nervous wreck. I was terrified and wouldn't let the person who took me out of my sight!

It wasn't until the BE conference 2010, when I found myself on the stage singing in the opening song, that I realised how comfortable I was, how much I felt at home and confident with my new friends. For the first time it hit me ... I wasn't pretending! I hadn't even noticed how much I had changed until I had this as a benchmark.

So what was it that had so drastically changed me, and so fast? I had heard the phrase "speaking life" in the church several times, but thought it sounded a little like self-help and psychobabble! I hadn't quite grasped the fact that it was just speaking as God would have us speak to other people about our situation, but also, most importantly for me, how I spoke to myself. Fortunately, it didn't need me to over evaluate theory or grasp the principles. Just being in an environment where speaking life is underlying every conversation and situation became kind of contagious and it was changing my life without me even knowing. I had come off all my medication; I wasn't so anxious all the time; I was healed of a 12-year eating disorder and I stopped self-harming. I'm not in counselling anymore – not because I felt I had to stop or it was a goal not to – it just happened because I simply didn't need any of those things anymore.

People in the church had accepted me, messed up as I was and regardless of my fears. They didn't judge who I was, they just told me who I am in Christ. They spoke a deep love to me and it showed me who I was under all that pain and destructive behaviour. They grieved with me over the lies I had believed and replaced them with truths for me until I was able to start speaking them myself. It's not a program of "10 truths a day keeps the funny farm away", it's just a (super)natural way of thinking and speaking in the language of God's truths. Nothing could be more simple, but harder too. It's well worth the effort of giving your mouth a spring clean!

Healing Testimony – Tom and Linda Wolstenholme

In August 2006 Linda Wolstenholme received significant prophetic news. At the time she really didn't comprehend its significance and so it was accepted, mused over, and then forgotten as life went on. The context for the news giving was a church summer camp in the beautiful English Peak District. During the camp Linda and her husband met separately with prophetic prayer partners through whom God foretold of future developments relevant to their lives. Interestingly, neither told the other what was said.

Specifically, Linda heard from God that she, "would go through some difficult things … it would be hard, but she would come through them okay and be able to testify and help others." In reality, God, through the prophetic word, spoke life to Linda at this point, though she didn't realise it.

Seven months later Linda had medical tests for some health issues and in April 2007 she was diagnosed with cancer of the bladder. Surgeons moved quickly to scrape out the cancer but found that it was still well embedded within the walls of the bladder (stage I). The cancer was found to be adenocarcinoma. This is extremely rare (just 2% of cancer sufferers have this type of cancer), very nasty and aggressive and this particular type of cancer was almost "unheard of in the bladder". To make matters worse, top doctors did not think it treatable with any form of chemotherapy or radiotherapy, believing the only treatment option to be surgery. Linda was fine with all this, as she was very anti-chemo.

It took some time for the size and extent of the surgery to dawn on Linda. The surgeons intended to remove her bladder, womb and ovaries. They then planned to reconstruct a bladder using a piece of her reshaped bowel tissue. The procedure was to take 12 hours and recovery to as near normal as possible would take around one year.

Before the actual operation Linda's prayer had been that the surgeons would open her up, see that there was no cancer after all, and stitch her back up. On 18th July the operation went ahead, but after three hours they decided to stop as they could see the cancer had spread to stage IV and believed it unfair to put Linda through such a big operation without it being a cure. They stitched her back up.

The day after the operation, surgeons told Linda about the procedure. They also told her how sorry they were and that they couldn't help her any further. She asked them if what they really meant was that they believed she was going to die. The answer was, "Sorry, but yes"! Linda's swift reply was that they might not be able to heal her but God could! The doctors advised that the original symptoms would reappear between that day, 19th July, 2007 and three month's time and would spread symptoms in other parts of the body in the following four to six months. The very opposite to speaking life was being spoken as she was effectively given six months to live.

Throughout all of this thousands of people were praying for Linda around the world, some she didn't even know. She was so very grateful. Importantly though, these people were also speaking life into Linda's situation through their prayers.

Having recovered from surgery, Linda later visited the hospital to learn that doctors wanted her to immediately start chemotherapy and then radiotherapy to treat the cancer they said was now in her bloodstream. Well, she didn't want it before the big operation and she certainly did not want it after the operation, and so it was declined! Everyone, including the church leadership and especially her husband, were encouraging her to have the chemo treatment. Tom particularly admits failing to speak life to Linda in these very difficult times and, as a practiced business negotiator, he used "every" means at his disposal to get her to have the chemo treatment. He believed that God hadn't said how He was going to get Linda through all this, healing via the medical or the miraculous, so he first begged, then required, bullied and even demanded that a twin track strategy be adopted.

Notwithstanding all of this, Linda held firmly to the prophetic words that spoke life to her in the summer of 2006 and so she firmly rejected ALL medical treatment. Her faith in God was absolute. He had said she would get through all this traumatic stuff, so she never wavered from believing she would be alright. When God speaks life, whether it is at creation or in the here and now, for a woman with a big faith, IT IS...

At the time of writing this article, over 4 years has elapsed since the big operation. She has had NO medical treatment! Yes truly, NO medical treatment whatsoever, and she continues to be fit and well, still surprising numerous doctors at regular check-ups as no symptoms have returned. Since the healing, she now obeys God by going out to speak life to others, especially cancer suffers, stating that what Jesus did for her He can do for them. Even this is a miracle, as Linda hates being the centre of attention.

(NOTE: This testimony is a personal account of a miraculous healing that Linda experienced. It is not intended to advise sufferers of any illness that they should not take the appropriate medical steps advised by their doctors.)

Finger Restored - Amanda Wells
My daughter Hannah chopped her finger off and we put it back on and taped it up. Bizarre as it may seem, we confessed one scripture repeatedly every day: "What God has joined together let no man put asunder." Though the finger was gangrenous and the doctors were intending to amputate it, it grew back from the top down and now looks as though there was never a problem.

Gynaecological Healing - Tina Holland
Some years ago my daughter was having a laparoscopy for unexplained gynaecological pain. While she was in the surgery,

I found myself walking round the hospital, almost like a walls of Jericho thing, praying life over her, for her fertility to be protected, etc. I really took authority and "tore down walls". The laparoscopy found nothing and her initial reaction was concern that she had no explanation for her pain, but her pain never came back either!

Pastoral Counsel and Personal Healing - Julie Gardiner

As church pastors we often see couples for marriage guidance. At one point we were seeing a couple every week and all we did was speak life to them as individuals and as a couple and it had such a great effect on them. Each counselling meeting we had with them they ended up being able to look at each other and laugh; their countenances really changed. However, because they wouldn't speak life to each other throughout the week, by the next session we were back to square one.

When I'm with people I often ask the Lord what would be life to them, and when I hear it, I say it. I'm often amazed at the great effect it has on them, but I was particularly blessed with one kid who was a friend of my boys. He had a reputation for getting into trouble, or rather, causing trouble. I asked him what he wanted to be when he grew up and he said that he wanted to be a fireman. I told him that was a great idea because he had the ability to lead people and was a very determined kid. I said that if he really wanted to be a fireman he could make that happen. The thing about speaking life is that it witnesses with people; they hear the truth in the statement. That boy's whole body language changed from a rejected, rebellious slump to a positive stance. It was so marked a difference I can still see it. I hope he made it.

My biggest example of speaking life was when I was really sick for over two years with a disease like M.E. For some months I was in a wheelchair, but I made the decision that I was a trinity of spirit, soul and body, and just because my body was sick didn't mean that my spirit or soul/emotions had to be too. It was really hard for the pain and exhaustion not to dictate my day, but I made a conscious choice to choose life. If I heard statements or even sighs coming from me that focused on the way my body felt, I would say out loud, "Shut up, Julie." Then I would choose to smile and focus on what I still was, rather than on what I couldn't do. It may sound daft, but I believe it stopped me from getting deeply depressed, which is a very common side effect of that sort of illness.

Husband Healed - Jenny Tremain

Bev gave me the early chapters of the new book she was writing about speaking life. As a company director I have been on many business courses where the subject has been positive thinking/ personal growth/getting the most from yourself, and I expected this to be similar with a Christian-flavoured twist.

I quickly realised it was different, involving a life connected to God in a way that I wasn't. I needed to look for and understand His perspective in situations, not to take the easy way out by agreeing with the majority in the everyday, general, negative gossip I sometimes allowed myself to get into. The words I read resounded in my heart and I knew I was learning important lessons for the way I lived, the way I thought about myself, and particularly the way I so often thought and spoke the opposite of life into my own life and sometimes others.

Some months later my husband David was told his prostate cancer was back for the third time. He had had two previous operations and we believed that the last one had been successful. I felt crushed. David is an impossibly positive man who shoves his feelings under a stone engraved "it will be fine", so you never know how he really feels, but I saw the disappointment in his stance; his eyes changed and spent time in the middle distance. The good news came when the consultant said he could have another Hifu operation. These operations are extremely uncommon, but the doctor felt it was worth trying. Hifu is a relatively non-invasive procedure that leaves less damage to the bladder, bowl and nerves.

David's treatment was in late December, 2010. I was sitting watching the snow when he came back into the room looking fine. I felt physically lifted by his smiling face. As the nurse left the room and closed the door, my love turned to me and cried hard as he told me the consultant had seen him straight after the operation and said it did not work and that he could not treat the area any further without damaging other organs and he did not think he had killed the cancer. There was a MRI scan booked for four weeks later to decide the next step. I held him as a well of pain opened in my stomach. My wonderful husband rallied quickly and decided it was not so bad. We went home.

In the next few days the pain I felt grew worse. David's options were radiotherapy or removal. Both procedures had the side effects of impotency and incontinence, but as long as the cancer stayed in the prostate gland the chances of cancer developing elsewhere in the body were unlikely. We were fortunate, but with all the intelligent self-convincing words and volumes of "it will be fine" from David, I could not shift the well of pain in my own heart. It was out of proportion and growing.

I tend to pray in the car. Sometimes it is more like a droning monologue of complaints or a list of requests, but whatever the shape that's where God and I do our stuff. Four days after the operation I was coming home from work praying and desperately asking for something. The words were disjointed; I was looking for peace, understanding, anything to move me out of this position of pain and hopelessness.

I thought about my friend's words about speaking life, getting God's perspective and faith. I realised I was scared to believe that Jesus could heal David; to believe meant going against the facts as they were. I felt I would be deluding myself and David into believing something that could not be true, therefore even if I believed now I would hit the bottom of the lake with a huge thud when the doc said David needed another operation.

The other ludicrous thing was that I felt if I had the faith to believe and Jesus did not deliver I would somehow hurt or bring down His name; it would damage the fragile faith I had and possibly David's as well. I remembered Bev referring to speaking life as being opposite to the common expression, "don't expect anything and then you can't be disappointed".

At this point I went the wrong way. Due to the dreadful weather I missed my turn in the road, which meant an extra 5 miles home. I didn't care if I drove all night.

God started to reveal to me what faith was. I had heard a thousand times that it was the opposite to fear. Fear is believing in something bad that has not yet happened, faith is believing in something good that has not yet happened. I thought I had faith, but on this "long way home" fear was an easy buddy. I reflected on the words of Bev's book and realised that if I chose faith, chose to believe in David's healing, chose to speak life into the situation and over David, it was better than the alternative of fear and failure. Go down fighting! I prayed into this, went home and told David.

Somewhere in the next few days I knew I really believed this. I took the first step and the Holy Spirit gave me the faith I needed; the pain had gone. David told me he did not have the faith for healing. As quick as the Holy Spirit on roller skates I thought, "Well people were healed in the Bible through the faith of others" and we both agreed that this was true.

On the day of the results the tension was physical, a few smart stabbing words passed between the woman of faith and Mr. "It will be fine". We sat in front of the consultant as he looked at the scan, and quiet and calmly he said, "Well, this is a lot better than I expected." The scan showed that the cancer had been zapped, well and truly! There was a tiny part that the doc was hoping was just inflammation and a MRI was needed in 6 months to be sure. But even then, if there was cancer left, it would be so small that treatment would be possible. I said lots of "thank you, Lords" under my breath until we got outside and I could whoopee loudly!

The 6 month MRI scan and blood test showed that the cancer was still hanging on, digging its heels into the small part that we had hoped was inflammation. When I first heard this my stomach did its usual dip into despair, but the Lord instantly brought to mind, "This is just procedure." My faith soundly in place, David will be having a fourth operation very soon and I feel confident in my Lord Jesus. The healing has, I feel, already been given.

Speaking life is not an easy choice, but the alternative is not an option.

Social Work – Sean Stone
I have been using the concept of speaking life in the work I do with Foster children and families. We tend to work in an holistic manner, since at times the whole family needs to be engaged with in order for a worker to understand the way in which a single family member may have problems. Speaking life into these situations has been a very useful tool for me and has worked to generate results that, to be frank, I may not have got using conventional social work theory.

I first learnt about this method while I was at a local church called Christian Growth Centre in Chelmsford. The way in which it was delivered made sense and the person who spoke about it was Bev Murrill. The more I heard about this and how it could be applied to almost all situations appealed to my inner social worker. After a few more times of hearing and talking about it, I decided to put it into practice in the real world, out in the domain of real families and real issues, among the people who are on the edge of society.

I had one lad on my case load at the time who I began to speak very differently to, using speaking life as tool to help him think about how his life was going and how things could change if his thinking and life application were different. Speaking life to him brought about subtle changes that increased. Over a few weeks and months his behaviour got better and although he still had blips on the way, overall things improved. I am not putting this down solely to speaking life as the solution, but in part it added to his perceptions of how things could be different using words that carried a positive influence.

I think that the message behind speaking life is a critical one and I have found that although it is simple to think about it, it is quite hard to do at times. This is partly due to the way we are. The issues we have may prevent us from communicating these "words" that are going to unlock a person's potential in a variety of ways.

Passport Control – Bev Murrill
My purse had been stolen and with it went my driver's license. I had to send my passport away with my application for a new license, which I did with alacrity, knowing that I was not due to travel overseas for the next couple of months and wouldn't need it. I forgot, however, that I needed to fly to Orkney from England and that such a flight needed current identification. My previous

experience with the low cost airline I was honouring with my presence was that a few years before I'd been refused the right to board the plane to Glasgow because my passport was just two weeks out of date.

On the day of my flight, after looking everywhere for my passport, I suddenly remembered it was somewhere between the DVLA and me. At any time this would be a big deal as the four flights between Orkney and Stansted are very expensive, but it was even more of a problem because at this time as we were currently in the process of some strategic negotiations concerning the future of the church and my visit this weekend was key in the proceedings.

I rang the airline and asked what they suggested. Their response was a flat "no chance, lady". As I explained the situation and pushed, they helpfully suggested that a driver's license ID would do. Once again, I explained that my driver's license had been stolen, which is why I didn't have my passport. Ultimately, the voice on the phone suggested a library card would do. Now veering slightly towards what could be called "late", we grabbed luggage and my 17-year-old expired passport and headed for the library.

Trying not to look flustered, I casually asked the librarian if they did photo IDs. The answer was yes, so I quickly filled out my form and waited (im)patiently for my photo to be taken. Fifteen minutes went by and they handed me my library card ... without a photo. "Don't you do photo ID?" I queried. Oh no, came the answer! It was one of those funny misunderstandings that I absolutely didn't have time for right now.

Off we drove to the airport, having called a few people and asked them to pray. I can't say that we didn't feel stressed because obviously we did, but we spent the 30 minute journey speaking out

God's perspective into my situation in the form of one of my most frequently used scriptures, thanking God that He is faithful and will always bring to pass what He intends (1 Thessalonians 5:24). We knew that He intended me to be there for that weekend of important meetings. Stress and faith make a curious and sometimes powerful combination.

Arriving at the airport, now much later than I'd wanted due to my diversion to the Library, I approached the ticket desk, carrying the passport I'd been issued when my children were in primary school and gabbled my dilemma to the official. He gazed at me without any emotion and said, "No, you can't get on the plane without current ID." I made another attempt to help him understand and inexplicably he looked at his colleague and then at me and said, 'Okay, I'll sign your boarding pass." I asked if he would sign the other three, the one from Edinburgh to Orkney and the two for my return journey. His face indicated that he thought I might be from another planet and he told me that I was basically on my own from there.

It was an astonishing experience. At Edinburgh my reception was similar. First I was told no, then without any real reason, the desk person changed her mind and signed my next boarding pass. I asked again if she would sign the others and was met with the same response.

So far, so good ... I arrived in Orkney on time. Without going into all the details, I found favour at every desk, only slightly complicated by the fact that upon my arrival in Glasgow, on my way home, there'd been a security alert and all the public had been cleared from the airport. My story was met with the same blank no and then a sudden turn around. I can't explain what gave me the favour I experienced with each airline official, except that God had gone before me as I expressed my faith in His ability to get me there despite my lack of current ID. It's important to say that at any point I could have turned back and I certainly felt the internal pressure to do so. The phone call to the airline, the lost cause at the library, the fear of getting the first okay from the flight official and then being stranded somewhere in Scotland and not being able to go forward or back. As far as I can see, the only thing that made the difference was Rick's and my refusal to speak the death of unbelief into the situation. We knew absolutely it could fail and if it did, we knew God would be in that, but we also knew that God had called me to Orkney that weekend and that He could get me there by a miracle, which He did, four of them! Two on the way up and two more on the way back!

Breakthrough in Poland – Jim and Sue Gibson

My husband and I went to Poland as missionaries before it was a member of the EU. Before we went we felt that God had told us to buy a house as a centre for His Kingdom-purposes and to buy a car.

As foreigners, we soon encountered many barriers to us doing this. But we continued to pray and speak out in faith that we would have a house and a car because we knew God had said we would! Even when circumstances looked like it wouldn't happen we didn't take no for an answer and saw God make a way where there wasn't a way as we continued to speak and act in faith. Within three months we had bought a new car and had it registered for a year. Within a year we had permission from the government to buy a house. We later heard from other missionaries and read in a Guide to Poland that it was impossible for foreigners to do either of these things!

"Faith (speaking life) doesn't deny the difficulty, but declares the power of God in the face of the problem!"

12
The Who
And The How

Becoming a speaker of life

"The only way to dislodge a mindset is to apply pressure."
~Rick Murrill

"We will act consistently with our view of who we truly are,
whether that view is accurate or not."
~Anthony Robbins

I am writing this book in my 60th year and the revelation of speaking life has percolated, simmered, marinated and soaked into me over the 38 years since I made the best choice of my life, which was to give my heart to Jesus Christ. More particularly, it has grown and developed since Rick and I came to understand that God has His own language and even though He can communicate with us in our language, if we are to become like Him as He expresses Himself to our world, we must learn to speak life also. Learning to do so has changed us, but it has taken time because changing the language you speak isn't easy nor is it common to make the decision to do it.

During the years since we became Christians we have traversed variously through stages of immaturity and lack of comprehension, through diverse forms of legalism, mysticism and various facets of Christian unbelief. By the grace of God we have continued on our journey of faith into the awareness of His amazing grace that set us free to live in the righteousness, peace and joy in the Holy Ghost that Paul talks about (Romans 14:17), not bound by legalistic doctrines nor hampered in our faith by an easy *believism* that has no substance.

Tough things happen to all of us, but it is our own propensity for sin that causes our view of who we are to become warped. As Walt Kelly's cartoon character, Pogo so saliently put it: "We have met the enemy and he is us." Our self-destructive actions stem from our internal compass going haywire. Our perspective is dictated more by our view of ourselves and our world than it is by our circumstances. This is why even when things are good many people speak disparagingly and cynically of their own achievements and other people's.

Our perspective is faulty. We need God to show us how He sees us so we can get His perspective of our own self and of our world. Perspective is what dictated the difference between what the ten other spies said about Canaan, as opposed to what Caleb and Joshua said. Perspective dictated the difference between how the Israelite army viewed Goliath in contrast to how David viewed him. Perspective will dictate your view of life and consequently your ability to change the atmosphere around you. Getting God's perspective on yourself first and then on the people you do life with is paramount if you want to live free from anxiety, stress, anger, self-pity, depression, pride and fear. God's perspective empowers you. Any other perspective, regardless of whether it finds its roots in your background or your circumstances or the people around you, disempowers you. In order to change the atmosphere over where you live and work, you will have to have God's perspective.

No matter what stage of life you're in, how long you've been living this way, or who has framed your world up to now, you still get to make the choice of how your future is framed. You have the right to shape your world, whether into God's plan for your life (Jeremiah 29:11) or not. This is your responsibility, but if you don't take it as an opportunity to bring freedom to yourself, someone else will write your future for you. That may be the person or season that has already caused so much damage in your life, because our hearts unconsciously lean towards agreeing with and maintaining what has been said about us. When you continue to follow through with those unhealthy and painful things, you not only agree with the people who said and did them, you are also giving them the right to continue to write your future in the same vein as they wrote your past.

It's ludicrous when you think about it. Why would we do that? Because it's so hard to change the way we think about ourselves and you can only do it with God's help.

An enormous amount of consistency is required to change the way you speak. It's not just about the words your mouth says. Changing your future involves reaching back into the furthest places of the history that is written in your heart and exerting internal energy to dislodge your belief system from what you've believed before. Changing the atmosphere requires seeing what Heaven is doing and doing it too.

Like trying to move a huge rock, it takes tremendous determination initially, often with little to show for it. As you continue to push, however, the rock begins to move. At first it's just a little, but if you keep on going, the constant pressure begins to bear fruit. Once you have the momentum going, the rock needs only to be guided and supported.

"Regarding the works of man, by the word of YOUR lips, I have kept myself from the paths of the destroyer!" (Psalm 17:4)

Changing your perspective of life and the world requires your perspective of God to be right. If you think that He has a vested interested in making your life difficult in order to teach you a lesson, you won't be able to change the atmosphere around you, nor will you be able grasp what it is to speak life. Every one of us has been hurt by other people on many different occasions – this is the "works of men" the scripture talks about.

The remedy? God's word in your mouth. As with all of us, David, who wrote this psalm, was hurt at times by people's opinions of him. When that happened, his identity teetered on the brink of being submerged under the junk of other peoples' negativity, just like it does with us. It was in those times that he used the word of God's lips as an offensive weapon, enabling him to keep himself away from the path of discouragement the devil was trying to take him on.

What God says about us in His word is more real and truer than what anyone else says. But we have to be willing to agree with Him, rather than with our accuser, even if that accuser is us. One of Jesus' greatest gifts to us was to throw the accuser down from our lives (Revelation 12:10), but that doesn't help us if we don't get revelation on that. We live in a blaming society. Finding someone to blame so that I can prove it's not my fault is common in marriages, businesses, churches, and wherever you find people working together.

If you want to alter the atmosphere in your context, it's vital to make the choice to stand on the side of the One whose finished work on the cross threw the accuser to the ground, rather than being on the accuser's side, adding your own accusations to his. Speaking life requires developing a *no blame culture* around yourself. Maturity and growth means fixing the problem rather than fixing the blame on someone else.

Speaking life is an interesting language in that you can't do it effectively and consistently unless you're prepared to give up your former way of speaking. If you're determined to keep your own opinion and not allow God to guide you in how you should think, you won't be able to speak life. You'll insist on speaking negativity into everything you do and everyone you work with, without realising how much you are robbing yourself and your world of the purposes of God as they could be expressed through your life.

If you are not interested in learning about the character of God or letting Him show you your own character, you won't be able to learn to speak life. If you want to keep other people *in their place* or you need to ensure that you keep your place as *top dog*, you won't be able to speak life effectively. Conversely, if you're afraid of being noticed or fearful that people might think you are putting yourself forward, you won't be able to speak life either.

Speaking life requires that you release your right to your own prejudices, biases, fears and pride.

You've got to change! You can't stay the same and speak life as well.

Learning to speak life and change the atmosphere over your milieu entails unlearning a whole lot of other methods of communication that you've used to survive and succeed in this world. You have to let go of sarcasm, being a drama queen, exaggeration, a superiority complex, self-deprecation, condemnation of yourself or other people, hurtful or negative humour or humour that shifts the focus away from the point, negativity ... these things are harder to weed out than you might think.

I used to be a master of sarcasm and a great drama queen. In order to learn to speak life, I had to make the choice to let go of these other ways of talking. It wasn't easy. It wasn't until I was choosing to let go of them that I realised how much I depended on them for my identity. Choosing to shut my mouth and not say the funny but cruel comments that made other people laugh (but cut someone down) was really difficult. It was even harder when someone else in the group said what I had chosen not to say and got all the laughs instead. Making the choice not to make a mountain out of a molehill was tough when that mountain would have got me a lot more positive affirmation.

I found quickly that choosing to deal with fear by looking for God's perspective and speaking life instead of spouting my fears to everyone who would listen, really worked. It was hard to do, but when I chose not to use the magnifying glass of the many repetitions of my story to anyone who would listen, when I no longer had the inflammatory fuel of other people's opinions on the fire of my situation, I found I got less sympathy but my fears were much easier to manage. It's amazing how fear and the drama many of us love so much causes our problems to escalate, or at least, to feel as though they're escalating.

If faith comes by hearing myself and others speaking the word of God, I realised that negative faith comes the same way. People often get into a cycle of repeating their fears over and over, enveloping themselves with increasing stress every time they tell their story again. Realising I was telling the same story three, four, ten times in a day made me understand that I needed to change the way I was talking. Bringing my crises and problems to God and speaking His life over my situations again and again, despite how I felt emotionally, began to work. The more I went to the Lord with my issues, the less I needed to get everyone else involved in the story. The more I took authority over the problems, refusing to allow them to dictate my life, the more free I became to live positively. As a consequence, the stories I tell have changed. They're stories of life and faith and strength and blessing, rather than of failure and fear and frustration. It's not that I don't have failures and fear and frustration, but they no longer dictate my thoughts or conversation and, therefore, they don't determine the course of my life.

When you hear stories about how speaking life has changed a situation, they always sound amazing, and they truly are. But a major aspect of speaking life is that it takes resolve to begin to do it and it takes courage to keep doing it. It also takes a willingness to trust God even when you don't see any initial breakthrough. It takes patience when nothing changes immediately and the understanding that you're building something new and different into your future. New things cannot be erected overnight. It takes time as well as insight into the bigger picture to see beyond what our current problem is.

If our efforts are about the one thing that needs to be fixed, we will forget about it quickly after it is fixed. Yet, we are often devastated and offended with God if it is not. We've all had times when we stood in faith but didn't see what we've stood for come to pass. The disappointment of times like that can be devastating. The only way to offset the faith killer of disappointment is to get an understanding of the bigger picture. It's about what you're building for the future. It's not just about this one issue, it's about a way of life that will not only change who you are and enable you to live a life of strength and purpose in Christ, making a difference to your world, but it will also serve as an example to help the people around you to know that there's more to life than just getting your every prayer answered ... although we all want our prayers answered.

"Hope deferred makes the heart sick, but a desire fulfilled is a Tree of Life." (Proverbs 13:12)

When hope is deferred too many times and we don't get what we were believing God for, it's easy to make the decision that it's preferable not to believe for anything rather than suffer the pain that loss of hope brings. At these times, knowing the character of God is imperative, because that will hold us together when it seems that everything is falling apart. You learn about His character through getting to know Him in the good and the bad, the failures as well as the successes. Giving up is too easy.

It's interesting to note that faith fulfilled seems to require more faith, rather than less. Instead of getting easier, sometimes it feels as though it gets tougher. Sometimes we have to stand strong for a longer time and that's often the point at which we falter. My husband Rick often uses the example of getting a stubborn lid off a jar. Sometimes I need his help to do that, because he's a lot stronger than me. But he says that it's not that I'm not strong enough – I'm just not strong enough for long enough! I can put enough pressure on the lid to dislodge it, but I can't keep the pressure on the lid for long enough to dislodge it. Spiritual warfare is like that. You not only have to be strong enough ... you have to be strong enough for long enough.

"Submit yourselves therefore to God. Resist the devil and he will flee from you." (James 4:7)

The word "resist" is the Greek word *anthistami* which is where we get our word antihistamine. The full meaning of *anthistami* is "to set oneself against, to stand your ground, to withstand." Your power to resist the devil is in direct proportion to your submission to God. The more you submit to Him, the more you are empowered to resist/withstand/set yourself against the work of the enemy. The problem is, you can't just make a one off submission to God to get your problem sorted out; submission is a lifestyle, and breakthrough comes because of the consistency of your submitted life.

"And let us not grow weary of doing good, for in due season we will reap, if we do not lose heart." (Galatians 6:9)

Being a spiritual being requires spiritual wisdom rather than the sort of wisdom we get from the newspapers or the TV. Many of us who are very determined people in other ways are inclined to give up at the first hurdle when it comes to spiritual things, simply because of the mistaken belief that it's all up to God and if He doesn't choose to answer our prayers, then He's the one with the issue. Yet we completely understand that we can't have a muscular body unless we spend time building muscle, and we won't be able to play keyboard well unless we spend time practicing. No one ever got up for the first time on water-skis and competed in a skiing competition. We are not endowed with the capacity to get things right first time, every time. Being a person of great faith takes practice and exercise to build spiritual muscle. It takes the decision to learn and speak the language of life. It takes the understanding that God has placed you in your setting so that you can bring the Kingdom of Heaven into that place.

And it takes times of failure to teach you how to succeed. If you allow them to, your failures will teach you how to do it right. If you know that you need lessons to help you learn how to operate in the spiritual realm, just as much as in any other realm, you will be more willing to go the distance rather than walk away in disillusionment when life doesn't go the way you envisaged.

Don't be afraid to fail. Don't allow someone else to write your future based on how they wrote your past. Don't give up when it doesn't work your way. Trust that the God who died for you will also teach you how to live. Make the decision to learn how to be strong enough for long enough. We were born for a purpose. Not one of us was ever called to be pew fodder, sitting around in the church, our only role to provide the bums on the seats. Tragically, many people miss their call. The grand plan God designed for their life never came to pass, only because they failed to understand that when God said "You!" it was them He was pointing at.

My heart grieves for all the aborted destinies of great men and women who were called to change their environment and now it's too late. The world is desperately sadder because of the loss of them, though they do not realise that. It doesn't have to be so with you. You can rise up even now and be all that God has called you to be. It's not too late. You can be the one who changes the atmosphere everywhere you go, bringing the Kingdom of God into your spheres of influence. You can be the speaker of the language of life that reinforces God's amazing plan for the people around you. You can be the difference-maker...

"For creation waits expectantly and longs earnestly for God's sons to be made known." (Romans 8:19 Amp)

Go on. The world is waiting for you. *What are you waiting for?*